BRADWELL'S

LONG

YORKSHIRE
DALES

PAUL HANNON

BRADWELL
BOOKS

Published by Bradwell Books
9 Orgreave Close Sheffield S13 9NP
Email: books@bradwellbooks.co.uk

All rights reserved. No part of this publication may be reproduced, stored in a
retrieval system or transmitted in any form or by any means, electronic, mechanical,
photocopying, recording or otherwise without the prior permission of Bradwell Books.

British Library Cataloguing in Publication Data: a catalogue record for this book is
available from the British Library.

1st Edition

ISBN: 9781910551622

Print: Hobbs the Printers, Totton Hants

Design by: Mark Titterton

Typesetting by: Mark Titterton

Photograph Credits: © Paul Hannon

Maps: Contain Ordnance Survey data
© Crown copyright and database right 2014

Ordnance Survey licence number 100039353

The information in this book has been produced in good faith and is intended as
a general guide. Bradwell Books and its authors have made all reasonable efforts
to ensure that the details are correct at the time of publication. Bradwell Books
and the author cannot accept any responsibility for any changes that have taken
place subsequent to the book being published. It is the responsibility of individuals
undertaking any of the walks listed in this publication to exercise due care and
consideration for the health and wellbeing of each other in the party.

These longer walks are for the more experienced walker with good map reading
skills, quality walking boots and clothing. They should not be undertaken by
walkers who have health problems that might prevent them from completing
the walk or compromise the safety of fellow walkers.

CONTENTS

Walk 1	**Lofthouse – Upper Nidderdale** 9 miles / 14.5km	**p.8**
Walk 2	**Bolton Abbey – Strid Wood** 9½ miles / 14.5km	**p.14**
Walk 3	**Burnsall – Linton Falls** 7 miles / 11.3km	**p.20**
Walk 4	**Grassington – Conistone Dib** 7½ miles / 12km	**p.26**
Walk 5	**Buckden – Langstrothdale** 9½ miles / 15.3km	**p.32**
Walk 6	**Litton – Upper Littondale** 7½ miles / 12km	**p.38**
Walk 7	**Malham – Malham Cove and Tarn** 9 miles / 14.5km	**p.44**
Walk 8	**Settle – Stainforth Force** 6¾ miles / 10.75km	**p.50**
Walk 9	**Horton – Upper Ribblesdale** 11 miles / 17.5km	**p.56**
Walk 10	**Clapham – Norber Boulders** 9½ miles / 15.25km	**p.62**
Walk 11	**Dent – Dentdale** 8½ miles / 13.5km	**p.68**
Walk 12	**Sedbergh – Winder and The Rawthey** 8 miles / 12.75km	**p.74**
Walk 13	**Howgill – Howgill Fells** 7½ miles / 12km	**p.80**
Walk 14	**Hawes – Hardraw Force** 7 miles / 11.25km	**p.86**
Walk 15	**Bainbridge – Semerwater** 9½ miles / 15.25km	**p.92**
Walk 16	**Askrigg – Whitfield Gill** 8 miles / 12.75km	**p.98**
Walk 17	**Aysgarth – Castle Bolton** 7¼ miles / 11.5km	**p.104**
Walk 18	**Reeth – Arkengarthdale** 9¾ miles / 15.5km	**p.110**
Walk 19	**Gunnerside – Gunnerside Gill** 8 miles / 12.75km	**p.116**
Walk 20	**Muker – Swale Gorge** 7½ miles / 12km	**p.122**
About the Author		**p.128**

THE YORKSHIRE DALES SITS AT THE VERY HEART OF NORTHERN ENGLAND, HALFWAY ALONG THE MIGHTY PENNINE CHAIN WHICH STRETCHES FROM THE DERBYSHIRE PEAK DISTRICT TO HADRIAN'S WALL IN NORTHUMBERLAND. THIS IS WITHOUT DOUBT ONE OF ENGLAND'S PREMIER DESTINATIONS FOR WALKERS, FOR IT EMBRACES ALMOST EVERY KIND OF LANDSCAPE, FROM LUSH RIVERBANK TO ROLLING MOORLAND. THIS RICHLY VARIED COLLECTION OF WALKS WILL HELP YOU DISCOVER AIRY HILLTOPS, HEATHER MOORS, GLEAMING LIMESTONE CRAGS AND PAVEMENTS, WOODED RIVERBANKS AND FLOWER-BEDECKED MEADOWS.

This beautiful area consists of a network of valleys all divided by high and lonely moors, and each with its own individual 'feel'. There are literally scores of dales in the Dales, with the principal valleys of Wensleydale, Wharfedale and Swaledale ably supported by Nidderdale, Malhamdale, Ribblesdale and Dentdale. Most of the rivers flow eastwards to ultimately swell the mighty Ouse that flows into the Humber Estuary. The latter two, however, flow west to enter the Irish Sea by way of Lancashire.

It is perhaps the villages that best capture the real Dales atmosphere, with Burnsall, Muker, Clapham and Bainbridge unquestionably some of England's finest. A string of such villages is ranged at regular intervals along each of the valleys, all looking like they grew out of the very land. Their charm is further enhanced by their setting among neatly packaged fields and lonely fells – a perfect backdrop. Second only to the villages are the waterfalls: every dale has some, from the lofty plunge of Hardraw Force and the celebrated trio at Aysgarth to other gems at Stainforth and Keld.

The past is never far away in the Dales, and the eastern half of the region boasts the coincidentally named Bolton Castle and Bolton Priory, while more recent history is evident in a lead-mining past that occupied thousands of dalesmen until less than 200 years ago. Farming of course plays its crucial role in maintaining the countryside as we fondly picture it, with sheep and cattle grazing among field barns, drystone walls, hay meadows and upland pasture. Most villages feature a welcoming pub or tearoom, while all manner of local crafts can be experienced including cheesemaking and brewing. When a little more bustle is required, the area is conveniently surrounded by a necklace of gateway towns such as Skipton, Richmond, Harrogate and Ilkley.

The Yorkshire Dales truly has something for everyone!

UPPER NIDDERDALE IS A WONDERFULLY REMOTE AND UNSUNG AREA OF THE DALES, WHERE EXTENSIVE MOORS CRADLE SOME LOVELY LITTLE VILLAGES.

Lofthouse is a small, tidy village high above the river, the focal point being the attractive corner which includes an impressive water fountain which bears words worth reading. A house opposite the memorial institute bears a 1653 date stone. The Crown Hotel refreshes visitors, while the little school serves all of Upper Nidderdale's youngsters. Alongside the school on the bottom road is the former station house, which was the highest on the Nidd Valley Light Railway.

Ramsgill is a visually striking village on the banks of its own beck just short of its confluence with the Nidd. Its prime feature is the spacious green, where attractive cottages and flowery gardens play support to the imposing ivy-clad hotel: this former shooting lodge of the Yorke family still bears their name. A circular pinfold stands in front of the village hall. The church of St Mary the Virgin was rebuilt in 1843, and looks out across the reedy head of Gouthwaite Reservoir. Ramsgill was an important grange of Byland Abbey, and at the rear of the church a solitary gable end remains from the monks' chapel.

Between Ramsgill and Bouthwaite the course of the Nidd Valley Light Railway is crossed at Ramsgill's old station house. Built to aid construction of the dale-head reservoirs at Scar House, it also operated a passenger service from Pateley Bridge to Lofthouse but was dismantled after serving its main function. Bouthwaite was an important grange of Fountains Abbey, less than ten miles distant at this point.

Fountains Earth Moor is named from its early owners, the monks of Fountains Abbey. This great upland stretches east for many square miles, an underestimated vastness of big, sweeping moors. It is criss-crossed by old trackways without a motor road in evidence save for the Lofthouse–Masham strip of tarmac, and even this was only made fit for motor traffic in the 1960s. These old roads were once important highways that linked Upper Nidderdale with its monastic landlords, but today serve only walkers, shooting parties and the occasional off-road biker.

THE BASICS

Distance: 9 miles / 14.5km

Gradient: Short, stiff pull out of Studfold and a longer sustained climb out of Bouthwaite

Severity: Quite strenuous

Approx. time to walk: 5 to 6 hours

Stiles: Two

Maps: OS Landranger 99 Northallerton & Ripon; Explorer 298 Nidderdale

Path description: Good field paths and firm moorland tracks

Start Point: Lofthouse village centre (GR SE 101735)

Parking: Lofthouse village car park (HG3 5RZ)

Dog friendly: Sheep pastures and moorland, so dogs on leads please; they should also be fit and able to manage the stiles

Public toilets: At start

Nearest food: Pubs at start and Ramsgill

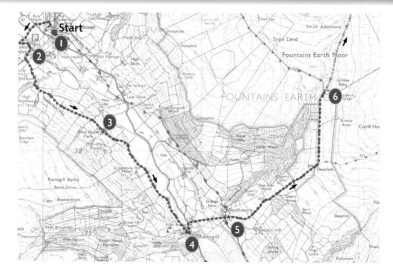

The Route

1. From the village centre fountain, take a gap in the corner of the square between cottages, and a firm path runs down a fieldside to a substantial footbridge on the Nidd. Immediately upstream are the beautiful Nidd Falls.  Cross to emerge onto the Scar House road, straight over to a kissing gate and on past the cricket pitch to another kissing gate onto the bend of a road. Go right a few strides then fork left on the lesser How Stean Gorge branch. This runs past a car park to bridge How Stean Beck. Cross and turn left to Studfold Farm. Once a small grange of Byland Abbey, an outdoor activity centre and a caravan site share the farming environs.

2. Turn sharp right up the steep, rough road to a line of cottages, after which take another walled track to the left. This runs on to cross Blayshaw Gill. Peer over the bridge, downstream, to view a narrow limestone ravine. Emerging into a field the access track climbs to High Blayshaw Farm, but your way advances just as far as a barn. Now head straight along a more inviting, faint but embanked green track to a stile/gate combination repeated in the fields ahead. The benefit of contouring the valley flanks gives this section panoramic views up-dale to Lofthouse, Middlesmoor and beyond. The way rises slightly, then goes on past a barn to soon run as a firmer track through the fields to West House Farm.

3. Towards the farm the path is deflected left, using stiles to see a neat snicket between houses to emerge at the other end. Resume on a track heading away, dropping though a gate and down to the valley floor. Crossing a stone-slabbed tiny stream,

the way at once swings back up to a gate and along a field bottom. By now the track has become a faint grassy way. After one further gate, and with the river close by, advance on to merge into an access track from Grindstone Hill House, just above. This now leads unfailingly and very pleasantly along to Ramsgill, with the river at arm's length down to the left. The village is entered by passing straight through a farmyard onto a small green.

4. Across the road is the main green outside the Yorke Arms. Turn left on the Lofthouse road, but immediately after crossing Nidd Bridge turn right on the narrow lane to Bouthwaite. En route, the course of the old railway is crossed. Passing a former Wesleyan chapel of 1890, the surfaced road ends at a track junction in the centre of the hamlet. For a very brief detour to see Bouthwaite Grange, advance a handful of strides further and take an enclosed access track bearing left between cottages to enter a farmyard. On the left stands the lovely old house with a 1673 date stone and mullioned windows.

5. Back on the route, go straight on ahead to a gate, beyond which a stony track scales the hillside. Halts reveal views back over the valley, including much of Gouthwaite Reservoir, while beyond Ramsgill the attractive side-valley of Ramsgill Beck tumbles from the moors. Nearer to hand, just above Lul Beck, a slate quarry operated into the early 20th century. When the gradient eases the going underfoot improves, rising all the way to Intake Gate and a junction at a wall corner. The track continuing uphill is the old road to Kirkby Malzeard via Dallowgill. Branch left to a second fork.

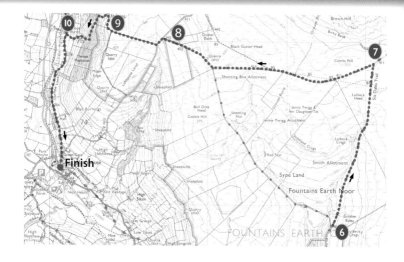

6. With a choice of gates, opt for the right fork, a modern shooters' way overlaying a historic track rising gently through the heather of Fountains Earth Moor. Sypeland Crags break the skyline across parallel Lul Beck. Higher up the track, beyond a gate, an inscribed boundary stone is passed to reach a T-junction. The right branch is the old road that engages several more upland miles towards Kirkby Malzeard and Masham.

7. Go left to commence a level march. At a stone shooting house, halt at the gate to identify Jenny Twigg and her Daughter Tib, two gritstone monoliths on the near skyline. Since the advent of Open Access, an appealing diversion might be undertaken to inspect these natural obelisks at close hand. Resuming, another junction is reached: keep straight on the main one, soon running out onto the moorland road to Masham.

8. Go briefly left and then take a gate on the right. A grassy wallside track heads away across a moor edge to arrive at Thrope Edge at the end, with magnificent views down over Upper Nidderdale. It swings right to quickly arrive at the unmistakable shooting house on Thrope Edge in a dip just ahead.

9. Immediately after the shooting house an inviting green path zigzags down the bracken flank to a gate in the wall below. This super grassy way was built to provide easy access from the valley floor – the farmstead at Thrope is now directly

below you. The path heads more gently left before swinging sharp right on reaching a wood. Doubling back down through a few trees and down a fenceside, at the bottom bear left to a gate in the fence below. Now head straight down a field to a gate by a barn onto the track behind Thrope Farm. Thrope is the site of a small grange of Fountains Abbey.

10. Turn left on the old way known as Thrope Lane, which leads a splendid, unerring, final mile-long course to ultimately reach a final gate just short of the Masham road climbing open ground just above Lofthouse. Turn down to the right to finish.

BOLTON ABBEY IS THE NAME FOR THE TINY VILLAGE WHOSE SHOWPIECE IS MORE CORRECTLY THE IMPOSING RUIN OF BOLTON PRIORY. DATING FROM 1154 IT WAS BUILT BY AUGUSTINIAN CANONS, AND AT THE DISSOLUTION THE NAVE WAS SPARED: IT REMAINS AS THE PARISH CHURCH. ALSO OF INTEREST IS ADJACENT BOLTON HALL, DATING FROM THE 17TH-CENTURY. AT THE START ARE A POST OFFICE/SHOP, TEAROOM, ANTIQUARIAN BOOKSHOP AND A SPLENDID EXAMPLE OF A TITHE BARN.

The Cavendish name features prominently hereabouts as this is the family name of the Dukes of Devonshire, owners of the Bolton Abbey estate but better known for their family seat at Chatsworth in Derbyshire. A tall roadside fountain commemorates Lord Frederick Cavendish, who was assassinated in Phoenix Park, Dublin in 1882. The Cavendish Pavilion stands at the entrance to Strid Wood, and offers all manner of refreshments, with a gift shop alongside.

Shapely Bolton Bridge marks the Wharfe's departure from the National Park, its peace restored by a 1994 bypass. A steam railway from Embsay runs to Bolton Abbey's restored station a long half-mile along the A59 towards Skipton. Near the bridge are also the sprawling Devonshire Arms Hotel and a tearoom.

Barden lays claim to the Wharfe's finest bridge, and a tablet on its east side dates its restoration 'at the charge of the whole West Riding' as 1676. Hovering above it, Barden Tower was built as a hunting lodge by the powerful Cliffords of Skipton Castle, and boasted two famous Cliffords as residents. Henry the 'Shepherd' Lord came in 1485, being raised in the Cumbrian fells until the Wars of the Roses ended. Up until his death in 1523 he preferred Barden's peace and the company of the canons of Bolton to Skipton's splendour. The redoubtable Lady Anne had the Tower restored in 1659 and spent much of her final years here. The adjacent chapel is now a restaurant.

The Strid is a dramatic narrowing of the river as it squeezes between gritstone banks. Lives have been lost here in attempts to leap the foaming waters. Many decades ago visitors could travel here in style by wagonette from the old railway station. Strid Wood is a very popular riverside habitat designated a Site of Special Scientific Interest. A splendid path network laid out in the 19th century has been well maintained ever since.

THE BASICS

Distance: 9½ miles / 14.5km

Gradient: Few gradients, undulating paths in and out of the woods

Severity: Easy

Approx. time to walk: 5 to 5½ hours

Stiles: Two

Maps: OS Landranger 104 Leeds & Bradford; Explorer OL2 Yorkshire Dales South/West

Path description: Riverbank and well-maintained woodland paths

Start Point: Bolton Abbey village centre (GR SE 071539)

Parking: Village car park (BD23 6EX)

Dog friendly: Dogs on leads on permissive paths, they should be fit and able to manage stiles

Public toilets: At start and at Cavendish Pavilion

Nearest food: At start, and at Cavendish Pavilion and Bolton Bridge en route

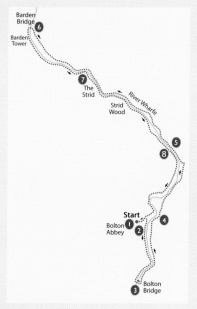

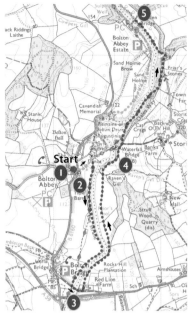

The Route

1. From the car park follow the short road out to a triangular green alongside the main road. Cross to a gate at the 'Hole in the Wall' and a firm path drops down into the priory grounds. On your left before the church and priory is the Duke of Devonshire's impressive Bolton Hall, dating from the 17th century. Follow the main path as far as a footbridge with adjacent stepping stones on the River Wharfe.

2.	Instead of crossing, turn right to follow the riverbank downstream. A long, pleasant pasture leads all the way to Bolton Bridge. As the old bridge appears ahead, the sprawling Devonshire Arms Hotel appears to the right. Through a kissing gate there is an option to cross directly to it, while there is also a tearoom across the road. A delightfully sited cricket pitch is passed to join the old road alongside the shapely bridge.

3.	Cross the bridge, and just beyond a cottage turn left along an enclosed pathway before Red Lion Farm, to enter a riverside pasture. As the Wharfe is neared the grassy way is deflected above a steep, wooded bank, and at the end it drops back down to cross long, flat pastures parallel with the river. After a tiny stream and a stile another wooded bank intervenes. A steep field is climbed, remaining with the left-hand fence to a gate at the end. Now go briefly left along the bank top to reach a superb high-level vantage point which reveals the priory ruins in style.

4.	Just a little further is a path junction. The main one slants down the bank to a T-junction, where the right branch immediately slants back up. Alternatively, simply remain on the bank top as a nicer, thin path runs on the wallside to meet the ascending main path. The excellent path quickly enters woodland, and runs a splendid high-level course along or near the top of the wooded bank. At the end it drops down to emerge onto a narrow road as it drops to ford Pickles Beck: a footbridge caters for pedestrians. On the other side a gate gives access to a riverbank path for the short stroll to a broad wooden bridge accessing the Cavendish Pavilion. Don't cross yet other than for essential needs.

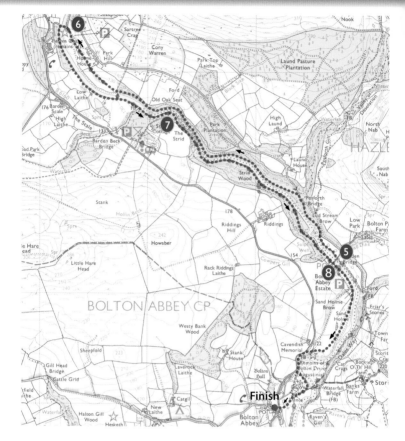

5. From your side of the bridge take the path upstream to continue. At a bridle-gate into trees it forks: remain on the riverbank, crossing a footbridge adjacent to Posforth Gill road bridge. The path clings to the river until faced with a surprisingly sustained pull to the top of the wood, where a well-sited rest house awaits. Bedecked with a luxuriant bilberry thatch, this upmarket seat occupies the first of several very well-chosen viewpoints. Hereafter, easy walking ensues on a magnificent terrace. One particular glimpse gives a surprise cameo of The Strid itself framed by foliage. Shortly after comes another classic moment, revealing the lively High Strid in a contrastingly open setting. The path leaves the wood to descend to the river alongside an impressive stone aqueduct built to carry a water pipeline from Nidderdale's reservoirs to the taps of Bradford: it also carries a short-cut path. Your path remains with the river to Barden Bridge, which is revealed well in advance.

6. Cross the bridge to the west bank, noting that a very brief detour up the steep road brings you to Barden Tower. At the bridge, meanwhile, a gate on the left sends a path downstream, briefly into trees before emerging for an open spell

back past the aqueduct. Entering Strid Wood remain on the main path, ignoring an early fork to the Strid car park. Other than at the Strid it is the woodland itself that steals the show from the river. Rising and wending nicely along past a viewpoint seat, after a steady pull to the wood top take a branch left running above a rock pinnacle – the Hawkstone – to drop down to the famous Strid itself, focal point of the wood, as the Wharfe is forced through a narrow gritstone channel of great depth.

7. The broad carriageway created for early visitors now leads gently all the way to the Cavendish Pavilion, a couple of late branches offering closer spells with the river.

8. From the Pavilion set off along the drive, but quickly bear left into the car park and follow an access road close by the river. When the track ends a path goes on through a gate, then, with the priory just across the river, the path swings right to climb to some steps to emerge onto the road at the Cavendish memorial fountain. Turn left to quickly reach a gate into the priory grounds. Now enjoy a leisurely exploration of priory and church before advancing on to rejoin the outward path to return to the village.

BURNSALL'S SETTING IS ONE OF NEAR PERFECTION, WITH BRIDGE, GREEN (AND MAYPOLE), CHURCH, INN AND COTTAGES FUSING TOGETHER INTO AN UNFORGETTABLE WHARFEDALE SCENE. ST WILFRED'S CHURCH DATES LARGELY FROM THE 15TH-CENTURY, WITH A NORMAN FONT. ALONGSIDE IS THE LITTLE VILLAGE SCHOOL, FOUNDED IN 1602 AS ONE OF THE EARLIEST GRAMMAR SCHOOLS. ALONG WITH THE RED LION INN, TEAROOM AND SHOP, THE DEVONSHIRE FELL HOTEL OVERLOOKS THE VILLAGE.

The farming hamlet of Thorpe has an elusiveness which long ago allegedly kept it hidden from the marauding Scots. At the centre is an enclosed, triangular green replete with springtime flowers. Romantically titled 'Thorpe in the Hollow', it shelters between reef knolls and below the overpowering Thorpe Fell. Prominent in the Linton and Thorpe scene, the rounded hills known as reef knolls are of limestone with a grass covering, relics of underwater mounds exposed by the eventual erosion of overlying rocks.

The riverbank walk between Burnsall and Linton Falls is one of the finest in the land; you are unlikely to be alone here but that is a small price to pay. The suspension bridge below Hebden celebrated its centenary in 1985, having been constructed to replace the stepping stones of Hebden Hippings which themselves have since been restored to use.

Grassington is the undisputed capital of Upper Wharfedale, a thriving community with a range of shops, pubs and cafes. While the cobbled square is the focal point, much else of interest is hidden down side streets and alleyways. Grassington boasted an 18th- century theatre and a lead-mining industry of which its moor still holds much evidence. Buildings of character include the Old Hall and the former Town Hall-cum-Devonshire Institute. Here also is a National Park Centre and the Upper Wharfedale Folk Museum. Immensely popular annual events include the Grassington Festival in late June, and Dickensian Saturdays in Advent.

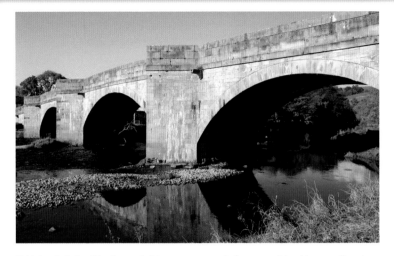

At Linton Falls the Wharfe erupts into a rare moment of anger as it tumbles over limestone boulders and ledges, a foaming sight in spate. In contrast, immediately upstream the river flows wide and calm between two weirs. Linton's church of St Michael and All Angels is seemingly remotely positioned, but central to the several villages it was built to serve. Dating from Norman times, it retains 15th-century work and its interior lives up to its idyllic setting.

THE BASICS

Distance: 7 miles / 11.3km

Gradient: Mostly level, with a few undulating fields

Severity: Easy

Approx. time to walk: 3½ to 4½ hours

Stiles: Sixteen

Maps: OS Landranger 98 Wensleydale & Upper Wharfedale; Explorer OL2 Yorkshire Dales South/West

Path description: Riverbank and field paths

Start Point: Burnsall village centre (GR SE 032611)

Parking: Village car park (BD23 6BS)

Dog friendly: Sheep pastures, so dogs on leads please, they should be fit and able to manage stiles

Public toilets: At start and at Grassington and Linton Falls

Nearest food: Pub and cafe at start, and at Grassington

The Route

1. Join the Wharfe by turning down between the Red Lion and the bridge, and follow a firm path upstream. It soon sees the back of the village, passing below the church and along to a knoll above the gorge of Loup Scar. Here the Wharfe rushes through an impressive limestone fault, a very popular short stroll. From these spectacular environs the path drops back down to the river to run through some lovely wooded surroundings to the airy suspension bridge below Hebden. Just before it, note the old stone stairway on the left known as the Postman's Steps.

2. On the opposite bank this uncomplicated leg of the walk resumes through a deep-set reach of the Wharfe. On emerging, a loop in the river is cut out by crossing a large pasture to the right of the tree-masked sewage works. Across its access road a

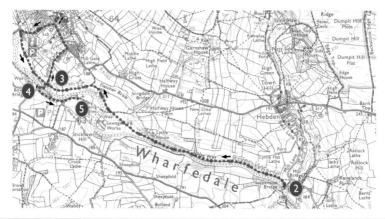

direct option crosses the stepping stones ahead to reach the church. If thwarted, turn right through the gate along the track away from the river and up past a fish farm. As it climbs through a bend, take a stile on the left to regain the Wharfe's bank opposite Linton church. A couple of fields further and the footbridge at Linton Falls is reached.

3. The walk will return to this point, but for the enjoyable Grassington loop turn right up the snicket (Sedber Lane, also known as the Snake Walk). At the top you enter the car park at Grassington's National Park Centre. From the road behind it turn briefly left to reach the village centre, with its colourful square on your right. Resuming, rejoin the main road which drops left with a footway to approach Grassington Bridge. Just before it, take a path on the left which runs beneath a row of houses, then drops down and on through a couple of fields. Passing a modern hydro-electric scheme and a couple of weirs it soon returns you to the footbridge at Linton Falls.

4. This time cross the bridge, and a narrow passage leads out onto a road. En route you pass the delightful Li'l Emily's Bridge on inflowing Captain Beck. Turn left past the car park/WC. To visit the lovely old church of St Michael and All Angels enclosed in a loop of the river, keep on to the road end.

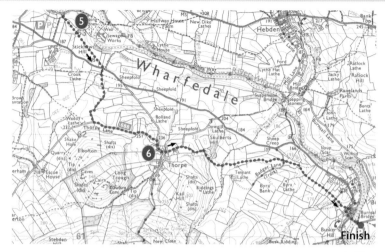

5. The onward route turns up a short enclosed way after the car park, before a house on the right. At the top a field is entered, and crossed to a stile just in front of the barn ahead. From it rise above the steeper drop to your left with a good view over the environs of the church, and cross towards a stile in the distant facing wall. Slant right across two slender fields to emerge onto the Burnsall road. Turn right a few strides to a gate opposite, and rise left to a gate in a fence at the top corner. Evident in the fields hereabouts are strip lynchets, the cultivation terraces of early farmers. Ascend again to an almost hidden gate, behind which a splendid green snicket wends its way up to join the similarly narrow Thorpe Lane. Go left into Thorpe, turning right at the end to enter the hamlet.

6. From the centre bear left on the road out, and a little further take a rough lane on the right. At its early demise descend a slim field to a small gate in a fence at the

right edge of a small wood. Resume away with a wall on your left, and on to a stile in front of a plank bridge on a trickling stream. The way rises away in a virtual straight line across three fields to reach the walled track of Badger Lane. A stile opposite resumes the fields' crossing, the immediate brow revealing Burnsall ahead. Dropping to a stile ahead, the

way slants right down to a corner stile, and a direct course for Burnsall is set. The church tower is a useful guide, while behind it, Simon's Seat dominates the skyline. More guidance is provided by a tightly bunched series of stiles, designed to test agility in addition to delaying arrival in Burnsall. The village is entered by way of a back yard, then turning right along the street back into the centre.

GRASSINGTON IS THE UNDISPUTED CAPITAL OF UPPER WHARFEDALE, A THRIVING COMMUNITY WITH A RANGE OF SHOPS, PUBS AND CAFES. WHILE THE COBBLED SQUARE IS THE FOCAL POINT, MUCH ELSE OF INTEREST IS HIDDEN DOWN SIDE STREETS AND ALLEYWAYS. GRASSINGTON BOASTED AN 18TH-CENTURY THEATRE AND A LEAD-MINING INDUSTRY OF WHICH ITS MOOR STILL HOLDS MUCH EVIDENCE.

Buildings of character include the Old Hall and the former Town Hall-cum-Devonshire Institute. Here also is a busy National Park Centre and the Upper Wharfedale Folk Museum. Immensely popular annual events include the Grassington Festival in late June, and Dickensian Saturdays in Advent.

Low evening light best reveals the traces of ancient rectangular mounds that are the old walls of an extensive prehistoric field system on Lea Green. Sloping limestone pavements and scars rise close by ahead, while Great Whernside and Buckden Pike form a sombre backdrop.

Conistone is an attractive little village avoided by the main road which heads up-dale just half a mile distant, across the river at Kilnsey. Even from this distance the famous Kilnsey Crag loses none of its grandeur. The central junction features a small refuge in which to relax beneath a tall maypole. A telephone box survives, as did a tiny post office into the 1990s. A pony-trekking centre operates from here. Every block of stone in Conistone's many old cottages matches the natural landscape of the village's hinterland. Though restored a century ago, the hidden church of St Mary retains some Norman features, though most poignant is a churchyard memorial to the six victims of the Mossdale Cavern potholing disaster of 1967 beneath the hills above.

Conistone Pie, an iconic little sentinel, is visible from many parts of Upper Wharfedale. From a distance it resembles a man-made tower, but closer inspection reveals natural limestone architecture boasting a marvellous panorama across the trough of Wharfedale to Kilnsey Crag and Littondale. Conistone Dib, meanwhile, is a classic example of a limestone valley, narrowing to very distinctive rock-girt termini.

THE BASICS

Distance: 7½ miles / 12km

Gradient: Fairly limited, undulating pastures

Severity: Moderate

Approx. time to walk: 4 to 4½ hours

Stiles: Twelve

Maps: OS Landranger 98 Wensleydale & Upper Wharfedale; Explorer OL2 Yorkshire Dales South/West

Path description: Good paths through limestone pastures

Start Point: Grassington village centre (GR SE 002639)

Parking: National Park car park (BD23 5LN)

Dog friendly: Sheep pastures, dogs on leads please; they should also be fit and able to manage stiles

Public toilets: At start

Nearest food: Pubs and cafes at start

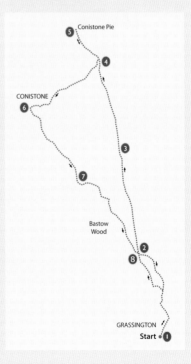

The Route

1. From the square head up the main street past the Devonshire Arms as far as a crossroads by the Town Hall, where you turn left along Chapel Street. Part way along turn right up Bank Lane, which quickly loses its surface and swings left as a walled track. Open views look to Grass Wood and the limestone pastures ahead. At a bend take a small gate on the left, over a plank bridge and across the field to a stile. While crossing, look right to note an arrangement of four parallel drystone walls appearing almost on top of one other. From the stile turn briefly left down to another stile on the right, with a rough track below. Here turn right along the field centre to a stile at the end. The next enclosure is the site of a medieval village, with grassy embankments discernible. Advance to the end and curve left to a stile in the far wall, beyond which a further stile admits onto Lea Green.

2. Head directly away, ignoring a path going left and also a left fork within a minute. Rising only gently, continue to ignore other branches (a major fork goes left) as your broad green way enjoys a steady rise to the brow. Now a parallel wall is seen to the right, though your path refuses to fully join it yet. The path finally crosses to a stile in the wall just short of the corner, and heads away to a bridle-gate beyond

an island outcrop. Rising through bracken to a stile, continue up past further outcrops to a huge limekiln. Constructed of immense blocks, like hundreds more scattered about the Dales it was built to provide lime for agriculture. Limestone and coal were put in the top, and burning produced lime for spreading on fields to reduce acidity in the soil.

3. The path runs on through the walk's high point to two further stiles, where it forks. Here bear right on the main path, rising slightly towards the head of the ravine of Conistone Dib. Reaching a gate, note that your onward route is through the small gate just down to its left.

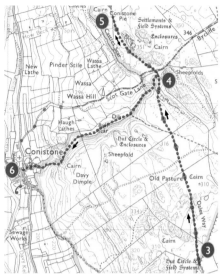

4. For an easy inclusion of the classic viewpoint of Conistone Pie, ignore this for now and pass through the main gate, and very briefly on between walls to a gate accessing the wide track of Bycliffe Road. Cross straight over and head off below a long scar which supports a superb limestone pavement with a limekiln at its far side. A stile is soon reached under the knoll of Conistone Pie, an iconic little sentinel visible from many parts of the upper dale.

5. Retrace steps to Bycliffe Road and down through the two gates to the small gate passed earlier by the head of Conistone Dib. Passing through, drop to a stile just below, where a wall abuts onto a cliff. The path drops stonily but briefly into the colourful valley head, which then opens out as you pass through a kissing gate to stroll along the normally dry valley floor. Beyond a further kissing gate the walls of rock close in to form the dramatic gorge of Gurling Trough, through which arrival in Conistone seems very sudden. At the end a couple of rocky shelves bring you out to emerge via a gate onto a green, at the end of which is the back road to Kettlewell. Just to your right is the church, while on your left is the village centre.

6. Leave along the back road to the left, and beyond the chapel turn left up a rough track. Through a gate the cart track rises right alongside a wall, through an intervening gate before rising more to the next gate. Early in this stage enjoy an impressive view back over the village to Kilnsey Crag, while below you is a good stretch of the river. The way now bears more to the left as the wall goes right, bound for increasingly colourful limestone country with Grass Wood ahead. Through a gate in a wall corner keep to the right-hand path to quickly reach an identical wall corner. Advance just a short way further to reveal the walk's next spectacular moment, as the ravine of Dib Scar appears at your feet. Dib Scar – or simply the Dib – is another dry limestone gorge, enhanced by a backdrop of woodland and of sufficient cragginess to attract rock climbers.

7. The path takes evasive action by swinging left along the rim of the dry valley, rising slightly to be joined by a wall. A little further, near the head, take a stile in the wall, across the low dip of the dry ravine and up the slope behind to pass through a gap in the next wall. Heading directly away with a wall to your left, a gate is shortly used to cross it. Back on the pastures of Lea Green, take the path sharp right, with scattered Bastow Wood just over the wall. Rising towards a minor brow a lesser right fork bears off; either option will suffice as this simply runs even closer to the wall. Both descend steadily as Grassington re-appears: the right one crosses a small limestone pavement before trending left above a better pavement, curving around to meet the outward route just above the stile onto Lea Green.

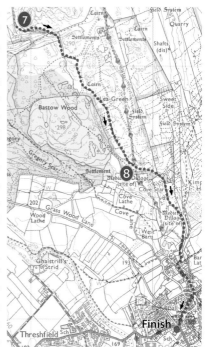

8. You can opt to simply drop down to the stile to retrace your outward steps into Grassington, or vary things for a little longer. If choosing the latter, then instead of dropping to the stile, go left on the track above it. This winds round above the wall to quickly reach a corner gate off Lea Green. A walled grassy way runs nicely back to rejoin Bank Lane at the point you left it on the outward route.

5 BUCKDEN – LANGSTROTHDALE

THE UPPER REACH OF WHARFEDALE IS KNOWN AS
LANGSTROTHDALE, WHERE THE YOUTHFUL RIVER WHARFE
FLOWS THROUGH FARMING HAMLETS EN ROUTE TO ITS
FIRST VILLAGE, BUCKDEN. IN MEDIEVAL TIMES BUCKDEN
WAS THE CENTRE OF THE VAST HUNTING FOREST OF
LANGSTROTHDALE CHASE, AND THE BUCK INN RECALLS
THIS FORMER IMPORTANCE IN ITS NAME. THE NATIONAL
TRUST MAINTAINS MUCH OF THIS PART OF THE DALE, AND
PROVIDES AN INFORMATION BARN IN THE VILLAGE CENTRE.
THE VILLAGE STANDS ABOVE THE RIVER ON THE SLOPES OF
BUCKDEN PIKE.

Your opening mile on Buckden Rake follows a section of the Roman road that connected forts at Ilkley and Bainbridge. To this day it remains an excellent route, and provides a perfect picture of the dalehead scene, looking beyond Hubberholme's church tower into Langstrothdale beneath high and lonely fells. The Rake looks down on the farming hamlet of Cray: situated at over 1,000 feet above sea level, the White Lion is a welcoming pub with a flagged floor, which was refurbished in 2015.

The section between Cray and Scar House is along short-cropped turf marked by limestone scars and sections of pavement. Throughout this stage you are treated to superlative views down the length of the dale. Restored in the 19th century, isolated Scar House was the scene of early Quaker gatherings.

Yockenthwaite is a classic farming hamlet in a magnificent setting, linked to the outside world by a slender bridge. 'Eogan's clearing' was named by the Norsemen who settled here. Much later, all this area was part of the hunting forest of Langstrothdale Chase. This small community once supported both an inn and a school.

Though barely even a hamlet, Hubberholme boasts two famous buildings connected by a shapely bridge. St Michael's Church is the highest in Wharfedale, and its interior features a 500-year-old oak rood loft, one of only two remaining in Yorkshire. Some pews bear the trademark of the Kilburn workshops of Robert Thompson, 'the Mouseman'. Outside, the sparkling Wharfe runs almost past its door. Across the river is the whitewashed George Inn. Formerly housing the vicar, its flagged floors are the scene of a long-standing New Year 'land-letting' event, featuring the auction of a 'poor pasture' which raised funds for needy parishioners. This was Bradford writer J.B. Priestley's favourite corner; small wonder that he chose to have his ashes scattered here.

THE BASICS

Distance: 9½ miles / 15.3km

Gradient: One steady, short rise in the first half-mile

Severity: Generally easy

Approx. time to walk: 5 to 5½ hours

Stiles: Twelve

Maps: OS Landranger 98 Wensleydale & Upper Wharfedale; Explorer OL30 Yorkshire Dales North/Central

Path description: Mostly grassy paths on lush limestone turf and riverbank.

Start Point: Buckden village centre (GR SD 942772)

Parking: National Park car park (BD23 5JA)

Dog friendly: Sheep pastures, so dogs on leads please, they should be fit and able to manage stiles

Public toilets: At start

Nearest food: Pub and tearooms at start, pub at Hubberholme

The Route

1. Leave the car park not by its exit; instead use a gate at its northern end from where a track gently rises up Buckden Rake, signed to Buckden Pike and Cray High Bridge. Through a further gate the way becomes stonier as it rises through scrubby trees: this is virtually the walk's only uphill stretch. At the end of the trees it turns right through a gate to commence a pleasant, level section. Ignore an early track curving up to the right, and further on also ignore a path bound for Buckden Pike which soon strikes off right.

2. Now a lovely grassy way, the accompanying wall drops away but your route remains foolproof. Just after the wall returns at a gate, take a bridle-gate in the adjacent wall and drop down a steep field alongside a wall: Cray's pub is directly below. At the bottom a gate leads to Cray Gill, which is crossed by stepping stones to join the road opposite the White Lion.

3. Leave Cray by a farm track immediately behind the pub, and follow it up to the left. Keep right at a very early fork to pass through a farmyard above various farm buildings. A little waterfall tumbles to your right as you cross its stream near the end of the yard. Ignoring a path signed down to the left, pass through a gate above the last buildings and your now sketchy way remains level through two fields before swinging right towards a barn ahead. Through a gate to its left, swing further right to find a tiny footbridge over the ravine of Crook Gill.

4. From the footbridge swing left to commence a long, exceptionally easy mile above a well-defined escarpment cloaked in trees on the left. Part way along, the Wharfedale Cairn beckons just up to the right: sentinel of the upper valley, this notable landmark is prominent in many local views. The only other interruption is a rare stile. All too soon the path arrives just above Scar House, which appears rather suddenly just beneath you.

5. Don't drop down to it but advance along the base of the open fell to a stile by a gate. From here a sketchy path sets an obvious level course through the minor outcrops of a limestone shelf. Throughout this section you enjoy largely level walking with some outstanding views over the youthful Wharfe in Langstrothdale to the Birks Fell–Horse Head ridge which forms a bulky wall opposite. Entering a small wood, the path quickly leaves by re-crossing impressive Strans Gill. Under this normally dry limestone ravine lurks a complex caving system. The path then drops half-left to a stile before commencing a level course through numerous walls in various condition. Further, beyond a bridle-gate, Yockenthwaite appears ahead, and a very short way further a guidepost indicates a gap in the abandoned wall on your left: from here the path makes a sustained slant to a wall at the bottom. It then runs on beneath trees to emerge via a bridle-gate onto a scarred track above Yockenthwaite. This takes you down to the farming hamlet.

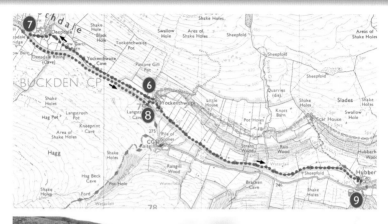

6. Without descending to the bridge, leave the main buildings where a guidepost sends a grass track to a gate to the right. At once a well-preserved limekiln is passed, and, with the Wharfe for close company, after a couple of fields the track fades as it passes Yockenthwaite stone circle. This compact group of 30 stones is of modest proportion but in a noble riverside setting. From a stile at the field-end beyond it, with a barn ahead, the thin path rises away from the river through a wall gap to another stile. Cross the field top to drop to a footbridge at the other side, then on through an old wall and a little gate to join the access road serving the farming hamlet of Deepdale. Turn down this to Deepdale Bridge.

7. This is the turning point of the walk. Across the bridge double back left along the road to Yockenthwaite. It opens out to run delightfully through open country alongside the youthful river. Within a mile you reach Yockenthwaite Bridge. Here leave the road as it climbs away towards Raisgill, and cross the bridge back into Yockenthwaite.

8. Without rising to the main buildings, turn right on an access track running above the lowest buildings. Pass through a gate and a couple more into the field behind, then down to a stile just below. From here a path slants down to join the riverbank. Note the lively appearance of a spring, swelling into the river from directly under the bank. The path now shadows the Wharfe downstream in idyllic surroundings, never more than a few steps from its bank. Passing through several fields, a

tighter enclosed spell opens out into fields again. Just beyond a barn the path rises a few strides to negotiate Strans Gill by way of a footbridge. An initially firmer path resumes, and at the end the path slants a little left to a wall-stile just above. A lovely final open stretch culminates in a rebuilt path across a steep, scrubby bank, emerging from some undergrowth to reveal Hubberholme's church tower right in front. The path runs on to meet the Scar House access track just behind the church. Turn right through the gate between church and farm to explore the tiny settlement.

9.   For the final leg of the walk cross the bridge over the River Wharfe to the pub, and turn left along the road, passing the attractive Kirkgill Manor on the left and Grange Farm on the right. After about half a mile take a signposted gate on the left to follow a wallside track to the riverbank. Here a firm path takes over, running a level course downstream through several bridle-gates to Buckden Bridge. Join the road to re-cross the Wharfe to finish.

Lovely Littondale runs just a few short miles from the old farmstead of Cosh to its meeting with the Wharfe near Kilnsey Crag; at Amerdale Dub the River Skirfare completes its journey having shunned virtually all publicity. Even its tiny villages see little of it, and only at the Littondale 'capital' of Arncliffe does the river flow by its church.

Several 2,000-foot fells close in, most noteworthy being mighty Penyghent. Littondale's flat valley floor and steep flanks replicate its parent valley to the east; indeed, from the vantage point of Conistone Pie above Conistone, they resemble identical twins.

Litton is only the second largest village (behind Arncliffe) in the dale of the Skirfare, but can boast it gave its name to the valley once known as Amerdale. Its attractive buildings are strung along the road from the whitewashed Queens Arms at the eastern end to a small green at the other end.

The ancient settlement of Nether Hesleden is the only habitation between Litton and Halton Gill, and features two 18th-century date stones. On leaving Nether Hesleden, majestic Penyghent soon appears ahead, followed by Fountains Fell above your return route to the left. A major feature of the walk is the opportunity to survey Penyghent from this less known angle, and this crouching lion oversees more than half of the walk.

Penyghent is one of the most impressive of the Dales mountains. At 2,277ft/694m it is the lowest of the celebrated Three Peaks, but is the only one on the Pennine Way. Additionally, its gritstone buttresses are the only place on the Three Peaks to attract the attention of rock climbers. As the hill is invariably climbed from Horton-in-Ribblesdale on its opposite side, relatively few people witness this quieter but still impressive flank.

The return route along the Dawson Close track takes advantage of an outstanding example of a green road, such an integral part of the Yorkshire Dales landscape. Like many packhorse routes it escaped becoming surfaced, and happily remains as one of the most distinguishable features of the district. At around 1,360ft/415m at its start, this highest point and turning point of the walk is a good one to linger over, savouring in particular the stirring prospect of Penyghent; the much less dramatic flanks of Fountains Fell also rise directly above you.

THE BASICS

Distance: 7½ miles / 12km

Gradient: One sustained but generally easy climb

Severity: Moderate

Approx. time to walk: 4 to 4½ hours

Stiles: Eight

Maps: OS Landranger 98 Wensleydale & Upper Wharfedale; Explorer OL30 Yorkshire Dales North/Central

Path description: Field paths, open hillside and a long, firm track

Start Point: Litton village centre (GR SD 905741)

Parking: Roadside parking (BD23 5QJ)

Dog friendly: Sheep pastures, so dogs on leads please, they should be fit and able to manage stiles

Public toilets: Nearest at Kettlewell and Grassington

Nearest food: Pub at start

The Route

1. From the pub head west through the village and leave the road just beyond the phone box, down a drive to the left before the last houses usher the road out of Litton. At the bottom the path runs on through a briefly enclosed section to a footbridge on the Skirfare. The river here is regularly dry, having sunk below ground some distance upstream. Note lovely Elbeck Hall alongside. Across, bear right to a gap-

stile just ahead, from where the path heads diagonally across two fields towards a pair of barns at Spittle Croft. From a gap-stile to their right cross the field corner past them to a wall-stile onto an enclosed track. This is followed right to quickly reach New Bridge, to which you will return near the end of the walk.

2. Without crossing, keep straight on to a gate in front, from where a rough track climbs the hillside. This old road is to be your return route, but for now make use of it only as far as a bend before it starts climbing, then break off across the field to locate a small gate in the wall corner ahead. Across the next field a small corner gate puts you into a walled section, emerging to pass right of a barn. Returning to the water's edge, this is not the Skirfare but Hesleden Beck just short of their confluence. Ahead is a first glimpse of Penyghent, soon to be much better seen. Several fields lead on to approach Nether Hesleden; a farm bridge conveys you over the beck, then through a gate turn left into the hamlet.

3. Keep left to pass between the houses to a gate from where two tracks head away. Opt for the one ascending steeply in front to another gate. Through this the track accompanies a fence as it rises above parallel Penyghent Gill. When the track shortly doubles back right, remain on an intermittent trod with the rising fence. A level section interrupts the climbing before a short climb resumes as the fence ascends to the fell road out of Halton Gill.

4. Turn left for a minute's stroll to a cattle grid, after which a thin path turns down to a small gate in the wall below. It drops a little further before starting a splendid traverse along the steep flanks beneath Upper Hesleden. After crossing a small ravine, ignore the grass track ascending right, and remain level to cross to a shelf to arrive beneath Penyghent House. Its enclosures are skirted to cross a mini ravine beneath a cave entrance. Just beneath you, Penyghent Gill is a lovely beck; unlike much of today's water this section is more likely to be above ground.

5.   Entering a larger pasture at a bridle-gate maintain the same course, rising slightly and going on through limestone to close in on the head of the gill. Across a rocky tributary, a grassy mound is the ancient burial site of the Giant's Grave. Don't pass through the gate ahead, but bear left to a stile near the corner, and advance along the wallside to join the open road by a barn. Turn left for a short rise to the start of the old road, which doubles back sharply left across Dawson Close. Penyghent truly dominates things now!

6.   Striding out on the old road, no further instruction is needed as it will lead you unfailingly back to New Bridge. Sometimes open, sometimes with a wall, it contours the flank of Darnbrook Fell for a considerable time before finally starting its brief descent, initially with an enclosed section. Litton appears ahead during this spell, which offers glorious views up-dale to Halton Gill, all backed by the great Horse Head–Birks Fell ridge. The outward route is joined just short of New Bridge, and either the opening half-mile or the rough lane leading from the bridge to the quiet road will lead back to the village.

MALHAMDALE IS THE NAME GIVEN TO THE OPENING MILES OF THE RIVER AIRE. THOUGH NOT ONE OF THE DALES' MAJOR RIVERS, THE AIRE ENJOYS FRUITFUL BEGINNINGS IN LIMESTONE COUNTRY BEFORE HEADING FOR SKIPTON AND THE TOWNS AND CITIES OF WEST YORKSHIRE.

Tiny Malham is a busy tourist village with 17th- and 18th-century cottages. The Listers Arms, the Buck Inn and cafes offer ample refreshment. In monastic times Bolton Priory and Fountains Abbey shared much of the land hereabouts, and reminders of their granges are found in the names of two of Malham's bridges, Monk Bridge and Prior Moon's clapper bridge. A National Park Centre stands alongside the car park, and the village has a youth hostel astride the Pennine Way.

At Water Sinks the outflow from Malham Tarn, for its brief existence known as Malham Water, disappears underground. It does not return to the surface for more than two miles, re-appearing at Aire Head Springs.

At 1,230ft/375m above sea level, Malham Tarn is an extensive sheet of water. Its existence in this limestone preserve is due to the layer of Silurian slate on which it stands. With adjacent wetlands the tarn is home to a rich birdlife. The surrounding calcarious grassland, woodland and limestone pavement further contribute to its status as a National Nature Reserve. It is jointly managed by its owners the National Trust and the Field Studies Council, who operate at Tarn House. The monks of Fountains Abbey held fishing rights here, while, as a visitor to the house, Charles Kingsley drew inspiration to create **The Water Babies**.

Malham Cove is an iconic Dales landmark, forming a jaw-dropping 300ft/90m sheer limestone cliff. It is hard to imagine the waterfall that once plunged over here after its journey down the Dry Valley immediately above. The top of the Cove comprises an extensive limestone pavement that is fascinating to tread, but only with care as the 'grikes' in between could easily snap a misplaced leg. In springtime athletic climbers must share the Cove walls with peregrine falcons that have nested here for many years; an RSPB observation post is usually sited on the path below. Issuing quietly from the base of the Cove is Malham Beck, which sank below ground on the moors above. At Aire Head Springs below the village it is united with other previously subterranean waters to form the 'official' birth of the River Aire.

THE BASICS

Distance: 9 miles / 14.5km

Gradient: Sustained moderate climb to Nappa Gate

Severity: Moderate

Approx. time to walk: 5 to 6 hours

Stiles: Six

Maps: OS Landranger 98 Wensleydale & Upper Wharfedale; Explorer OL2 Yorkshire Dales South/West

Path description: Mostly good paths on limestone turf, also a limestone pavement

Start Point: Malham village centre (GR SD 900626)

Parking: National Park car park (BD23 4DG)

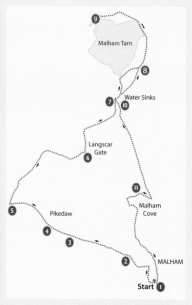

Dog friendly: Sheep pastures, so dogs on leads please, they should be fit and able to manage stiles

Public toilets: At start

Nearest food: Pubs and cafes in village; refreshment van often at Water Sinks Gate

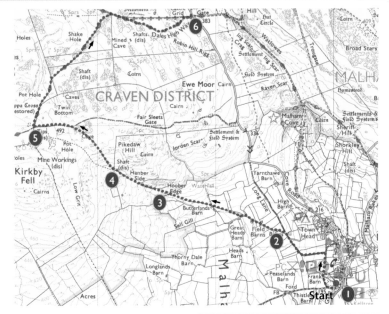

The Route

1. From the car park entrance don't join the road into the village but turn up a walled track on the right, then right again almost immediately on a similar track. Ignore a grassy branch left opposite a barn and take the next track climbing to the left. On levelling out it forks at a water treatment works, and your way is the main one, left. Malham Cove is well seen across to the right, while Kirkby Fell and Pikedaw rise steeply ahead.

2. After a slab footbridge and ford leave the track by a wall-stile on the right, and cross to a prominent barn, re-crossing the stream en route at a simple bridge by a wall corner. From a stile by the barn a path heads up the field, at once crossing a tiny stream, and keeping above the beck to reach a gate/stile at the top. Note the line of the Mid-Craven Fault along

the course of the beck. The hills ahead also emphasize this marked transition from gritstone to limestone, as Kirkby Fell exhibits the former and Pikedaw the latter.

3.   Once height has been gained on leaving Malham, look back over the village to see, to particularly good advantage, the lynchets across the hillside. These are the ancient cultivation terraces of Anglian farmers, providing level strips to produce crops on steep slopes. The path maintains the same line, soon crossing the tiny stream to ascend parallel with its trough on your right. Passing an old spoil heap it levels out to reach a stile in the wall ahead. Pikedaw Hill's crest is a steep pull to the right, though most of its view can be savoured from your path.

4.   Resume straight up the slope in front beneath low limestone scars on your right, while looking across to the gritstone boulders on Kirkby Fell. After a short, steeper pull the gradient eases and the path swings right up onto grassy moorland. Part way along is a neat glimpse of the mighty crouching lion of Penyghent through a gap ahead. A quad track is crossed as the path ascends gently to the prominent Nappa Gate, passing pools and spoil heaps from 19th-century calamine workings on the way. Just before merging with a broader bridle-track at the gate, a covered shaft is seen just to the right, by the track. By the time the walk's summit of around 1,689ft/515m is gained at Nappa Gate, the view embraces Malham Tarn, with Buckden Pike and Great Whernside beyond.

5.   On passing through Nappa Gate turn sharp right on a grassy wallside path for two minutes to the wall corner at Nappa Cross. This is one of several wayside crosses in the area, a guidepost for travellers since monastic times. Set into the wall, the restored shaft stands in its original base. Ahead is a fine prospect of Malham Tarn in its upland bowl. Beyond the cross a broad grassy way slopes down to a gate, and maintains this slant through further moor-grass pastures to meet the grassy Gorbeck Road at a wall corner. Turn right down this to descend close by a wall to a road by a cattle grid at Langscar Gate.

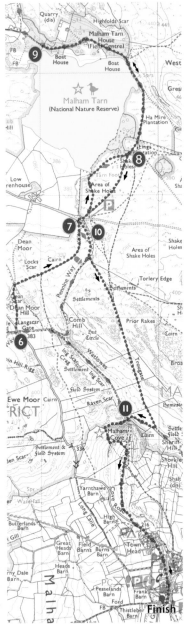

6. Turn left over the grid and advance just a short way before bearing off to the right on a bridleway. It meanders along to an old gateway in a wall, through which it heads directly away before swinging left to then drop down towards the stream of Malham Water just above its departure underground at Water Sinks. You will return to Water Sinks after a visit to the Tarn, so for now continue along to the left the very short way to a kissing gate onto the road at Water Sinks Gate.

7. Turn right through the gate to a large car park on the left. From the rear of the car park a path sets off across the moor. Immediately forking, the left branch runs on to quickly reach Tarn Foot, where Malham Water emerges from Malham Tarn, a spot to linger. Turn right on a path above the shore to the top end of a walled wood, and on to merge with an access road at a gate.

8. Pass through and follow this drive along the shore of the tarn, passing the cliffs of Great Close Scar. Entering woodland, the drive runs on to Malham Tarn House. Passing around its rear the continuing access road squeezes between rock walls to reach a tarn viewpoint and then a bird hide on the left. With its splendid vantage point over the water and into its reedy shores, this is the turning point.

9. Retrace your steps to the gate at the entrance back onto the grassy moor, and then bear right on a green path, past the wood corner to cross the moor back to Water Sinks Gate, and then continue back to Water Sinks itself.

10. Immediately behind Water Sinks is a wall-stile. Across this a grassy path rises away with a wall to the left, quickly reaching a path crossroads alongside some pools on Prior Rakes. This extensive sheep pasture recalls the landowning interests of Fountains Abbey: the former dewponds were created to help slake their cattle's thirst in these limestone uplands. Turn right here along the far edge of the pools, and a broad path rises gently to a hidden stile in the next wall. From here you pass through the well-defined trench of Trougate between low limestone outcrops. Through an old wall and then down to a ladder-stile in the next wall, another path junction is reached. Turn right down the wallside to a bridle-gate in the wall at the top of Malham Cove. The extensive limestone pavement is fascinating to tread, but with care as the grikes in between have great leg-damaging capabilities. Be aware also that the Cove's unguarded cliff falls 300 feet.

11. Turn right to the far end of the pavement, where a kissing gate sends a stepped path down the slopes at the end of the Cove. At the bottom, bear left to appraise the base of the mighty cliff. Issuing from it is Malham Beck, having sunk higher on the moor: rock climbers may be in action above you. To return to Malham turn downstream on the broad path through fields to emerge onto the road at Town Head, featuring the National Trust's Townhead Barn: go left for the village centre.

THE BUSTLING LITTLE TOWN OF SETTLE IS AN IMPORTANT FOCAL POINT FOR AN EXTENSIVE RURAL AREA, AND IS A LONG-ESTABLISHED HALTING PLACE. MARKET DAY PRESENTS THE LIVELIEST SCENE, WHEN EACH TUESDAY THE SMALL SQUARE IS AWASH WITH COLOUR. SHOPS, PUBS AND CAFES ARE SPREAD BETWEEN NUMEROUS INTERESTING BUILDINGS: FACING THE SQUARE IS THE HISTORIC ROW KNOWN AS THE SHAMBLES, WITH SHOPS PEEPING FROM BEHIND ARCHWAYS. NEARBY IS THE 17TH-CENTURY FOLLY WITH A SPECTACULARLY INTRICATE FACADE, NOW HOME TO THE MUSEUM OF NORTH CRAVEN LIFE. FACING THE SQUARE IS A FORMER INN, 'THE NAKED MAN', ITS CARVED SIGN OF 1633 WELL PLACED TO SPARE HIS BLUSHES.

Stackhouse huddles beneath a hillside, happy to remain hidden in protective greenery. The River Ribble at nearby Locks is a good place to appraise 19th-century Dales industry: from the footbridge you look down on the weir that supplied the adjacent millpond that provided water for the large mill at the other end, while alongside are rows of cottages that would have been occupied by millworkers.

Stainforth village stands high above the Ribble. Centrally located is the Craven Heifer, while around the corner is St Peter's Church. Stainforth's best-known features are its packhorse bridge and Stainforth Force on the Ribble. The idyllically sited falls are a rare burst of activity for the normally sedate Ribble, while the graceful 17th-century Stainforth Bridge was built to serve the York to Lancaster packhorse trade.

Langcliffe is a delightful village spread alongside a spacious green. Opposite the phone box a tablet on a house wall depicts the Naked Woman, modestly dated 1660: once an inn, it was a close friend of Settle's more famous Naked Man. The church of St John the Evangelist overlooks the green, while assorted cottages sit back from the war memorial fountain.

The Craven Lime Works is a fascinating site of industrial archaeology. Focal point is the iconic Hoffman Kiln, the most impressive limekiln in the country. Constructed in 1873, it features an amazing 22 individual chambers, all with their own arches but opened out, on a scale that could hold an indoor chariot race. Working around the clock, at its peak the kiln's demands occupied 90 workers as, fired by coal, it produced high-quality lime from the quarried stone for use in various industrial processes. Alongside is a tunnel entrance through which horse-drawn waggons brought limestone blocks out of the quarry above.

THE BASICS

Distance: 6¾ miles / 10.75km

Gradient: Minimal

Severity: Easy

Approx. time to walk: 3½ to 4½ hours

Stiles: Twelve

Maps: OS Landranger 98 Wensleydale & Upper Wharfedale; Explorer OL2 Yorkshire Dales South/West

Path description: Riverbank and field paths

Start Point: Settle town centre (GR SD 819636)

Parking: Central car parks (BD24 9RH)

Dog friendly: Sheep pastures, so dogs on leads please, they should be fit and able to manage stiles

Public toilets: At start and at Stainforth

Nearest food: Pubs and cafes at start, pub at Stainforth

The Route

1. From the Town Hall by the market place cross the main road and head down Kirkgate, passing the Friends' Meeting House. Under the railway bridge keep straight on, passing a supermarket on the left. At the bend leave the road and take a footway left of the fire station. At the end swing right to pass around the back of Kings Mill, now converted to residential use. Go left to a footbridge over the River Ribble and turn upstream on a footway to Settle Bridge, the main road bridge.

2. Cross the road and head straight off along an enclosed path between sports fields: ahead, Penyghent looks magnificent. At the end join the river

briefly before being ushered away into a field. Cross to a prominent gap-stile to enjoy a good section above a steep wooded riverbank. Emerging again, bear left to a stile just beyond a gate onto Stackhouse Lane. Turn right to the edge of Stackhouse.

3. A short loop gives a slightly closer look at Stackhouse; take the first rough road into it, turning first right along what becomes a grassy cart track, then right again back onto the road. Just a few strides further, take a walled green path to the right alongside a solitary house at Ribblelands. This runs to meet the Ribble at Locks, an attractive scene that incorporates old millworkers' cottages, a millpond, and a weir and footbridge on the Ribble.

4. Don't cross the footbridge but turn immediately upstream with the river. Your riverside stroll runs through several pastures leading to a longer stretch opposite the former mill. The steep wooded bank on your left is richly carpeted in springtime with wild garlic. A little further on you are briefly parted from the Ribble, climbing a few steps to a wall-stile then on past a lively spring. From a stile beyond it, advance along a firm, level path into new tree plantings, on through a bridle-gate and between further plantings to a gate at the end. With the river alongside again, instead take the bridle-gate to the right to regain the bank just beyond a confluence with Stainforth Beck. Just a few paces further on you reach the delightful waterplay of Stainforth Force, very much a place to linger.

5. Just beyond the falls you join a narrow back road at Stainforth Bridge. Cross this and ascend the steep, narrow lane. Immediately before it bridges the railway to join the valley road, instead take a gate on the right, and an enclosed path runs parallel with the railway before dropping left to cross it on a high bridge. Again just before joining the road, take a bridle-gate on the right and a path drops into a small enclosure, then uses an underpass beneath the road alongside Stainforth Beck to emerge into the car park.

6.   From its entrance turn right on the road into the village centre, then right again to bridge Stainforth Beck to reach the pub. Continue past it along the street to rejoin the valley road. Just a short way along the footway take a stile on the left and head along the field to a gate/stile. Stainforth Scar is cloaked in trees up to the left. Continue on towards the end of the next field where a fence-stile puts you into the environs of the former Craven Lime Works. A short choice awaits here. Either go left for the old winding house and then down an incline, or right for the massive triple draw kilns of 1872. The paths rejoin beyond them to run to a wall-stile across a slab bridge, now revealing the amazing Hoffman Kiln in front, deserving of exploration.

7.   At the far end of the kiln drop down into a car park. Pass to the left of the house and follow the access road out, passing another car park and a red-brick weigh house. Just after this a short path detours back left up to the remains of the Spencer Kilns, which produced a purer form of lime. Just further the road swings right to pass under the railway to join the valley road. Don't pass under the bridge, however, but take an enclosed cart track on the left on the near side of the line. Through a gate/stile at the end the track emerges into a field. Undulating pleasantly along towards the far side, as it turns uphill keep

straight on to a stile just ahead. A thinner path takes up the running, crossing to a stile on a gentle brow. Look back here to appraise a fine prospect up the valley. Continue to a stile ahead, then bear left across to a corner stile onto a grassy lane. Turn right on this, the short way into Langcliffe.

8. Turn left, with the green on your right, and as the road leaves the village by passing through a gateway prior to climbing away, instead take a gate to the right. A path ascends steeply to a gate at the top. Bear right from here on a thin, lower path above a wall, now levelling out. Beyond a bridle-gate, advance on to a gate by converging walls to merge with another bridleway from the left. On again, becoming briefly enclosed, Settle is laid out as on a map. Following a wall to a gate at the end, the enclosed Banks Lane descends onto a back lane at the top of Constitution Hill. Turn left to drop back into the centre.

HORTON-IN-RIBBLESDALE IS THE FIRST VILLAGE IN A VALLEY WHICH ENDS IN THE IRISH SEA BEYOND PRESTON, AND IS VERY MUCH THE CENTRE OF THREE PEAKS COUNTRY. IT HAS LITTLE INTRINSIC CHARM, BEING A MIXTURE OF DWELLINGS STRUNG ALONG THE ROAD, AND OVERLOOKED BY A LARGE QUARRY. SEVERAL COTTAGE DATE STONES GO BACK TO THE LATE 17TH-CENTURY.

Horton's real attraction is its location: there is a true walkers' atmosphere here. There is a popular campsite and a renowned cafe that caters for the weary, while pubs are found at either end. The Crown has two arched bridges outside, while the Golden Lion faces St Oswald's Church with its Norman doorway and its slightly leaning tower.

Selside is known more for nearby Alum Pot than for its own charms, although this quiet hamlet contains some nice corners. It once boasted an inn, the Red Lion, and centuries earlier, in keeping with much of the land hereabouts, was in the hands of the Cistercian monks of distant Furness Abbey.

Alum Pot is one of the great names of the Yorkshire underworld, and its system offers more than most for those of us who prefer to keep the sky in view. The general picture is that water from Upper Long Churn travels underground, becoming exposed for the final yards to Diccan Pot; from here it runs to enter Alum Pot part way down its  vertical shaft. Lower Long Churn interrupts things with the stream failing to surface fully. Explorations without experience or equipment remain, however, limited to forays near the entrances (but not Alum Pot's gaping one!). Immediately above this area the moor turns a sombre brown, its lofty wall rising to Ingleborough's sidekick Simon Fell.

The limestone pavements of Thieves Moss and Moughton Scars are truly magnificent, and the walk around their rim is further enhanced by long views down into the green bowl of Crummack Dale, a beautiful upland valley wedged between the limestone bulwarks of Moughton and Norber.

A major feature for much of the walk is Penyghent, one of the most impressive of the Dales mountains and completely dominating this part of Ribblesdale and much of this walk. At 2,277ft/694m it is the lowest of the celebrated Three Peaks, but is the only one on the Pennine Way. Additionally, its gritstone buttresses are the only place on the Three Peaks to attract the attention of rock climbers.

THE BASICS

Distance: 11 miles / 17.5km

Gradient: Long steady rise at outset

Severity: Moderate

Approx. time to walk: 5½ to 6½ hours

Stiles: Seventeen

Maps: OS Landranger 98 Wensleydale & Upper Wharfedale; Explorer OL2 Yorkshire Dales South/West

Path description: Mostly good field paths, also limestone pavements and a stony track

Start Point: Horton village centre (GR SD 808726)

Parking: Village car park (BD24 0HG)

Dog friendly: Sheep pastures, so dogs on leads please, they should be fit and able to manage stiles

Public toilets: At start

Nearest food: Pubs and cafe at start

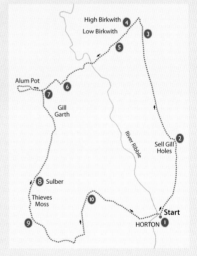

Start

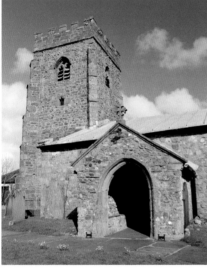

The Route

1. Leave the village by the rough Harber Scar Lane up the far side of the Crown Hotel. It soon improves to rise steadily away as a classic Dales green lane. Within a minute Ingleborough appears, followed swiftly by Penyghent, on whose slopes you are walking, and before long the third Three Peak, Whernside, appears set unobtrusively further back. With no complications the track eventually runs part-unenclosed to the grassy environs of Sell Gill Holes. Here are a stream entrance and a dry pot, with an apparently monstrous cavern below (don't try to find it though!).

2.   Through the gate behind, the broad track of the Pennine Way is left by crossing to a stile just along to the left. The main track continuing on up the open moor is the Settle–Langstrothdale packhorse route. From the stile go past the barn and turn at once through a gate on the right, to commence a long, level walk on a broad shelf. After a couple of stiles a broad grassy way continues through a long, rougher pasture, at the end of which you advance through two successive gates to a ladder-stile just ahead beneath a ruinous limekiln. The (invisible) path forks here, but maintain your course, rising slightly to a ladder-stile/gate in the next wall ahead. The path returns in a thistly pasture to arrive unannounced at a surprisingly deep-cut ravine.

3.   Descend cautiously to a ladder-stile in the bottom, then up the other side and on as before. Approaching a plantation the path swings up to the right to a small limestone pavement, then advance on above a wood containing Birkwith Cave to merge into a stony track from the right. Go left to a gate/stile and along the wallside track to a junction just below Old Ing. Turn down the stony road to a gate into High Birkwith Farm, once a packmans' inn on the Settle–Hawes trail.

4.   Here the terminus of the road from Horton is joined, but only for 30 paces before taking a wall-stile on the right. Bear left down to stiles in and out of a strip plantation, the way emerging to aim for the farm at Low Birkwith below. Joining the wall below, follow it left to a stile in a recess. Then drop towards the farm, past sheep pens to a gate where a grassy way runs alongside Coppy Gill to the yard at the front of the house.

5.   Advance to a wall-stile in a grassy corner enclosure, then to another just ahead across a track. Keeping all buildings to the left, advance on again close by the beck, passing the last of the barns as a gate puts you out into a field. Continue on outside the beck's wooded confines. One more wall-stile precedes a simple bridge across the stream to gain access to a wooden footbridge across the Ribble itself. From a small gate on the other side swing around the base of the knoll behind, and a corner gate/stile at the head of a walled lane is reached. Drain Mires Lane strikes unerringly up into Selside.

6. After passing under the railway, the white-walled Selside Farm is passed on the right. As Alum Pot and its neighbours are situated wholly on private land, this is the place to pay your nominal fee if wishing to explore the environs of Alum Pot, just a little further ahead. Whether doing so or not, on reaching the green turn right along the main road, out of the hamlet and then quickly left along a rough lane. At its far end a contrasting green lane strikes off left, and this is the continuation of the route. In front is a gate/stile, so if you've paid your cash, set off to explore the wonders of cave country. From the stile a broad path leads directly up to the mighty Alum Pot, tree-shrouded and walled.

7. Access to the hole is by a stile in its surrounding wall, though extreme care is needed as the main drop is a sheer 200ft/60m. Above it a thin path slants across to Diccan Pot, above which is Long Churn Pot. Going round by the wall to a stile, Upper Long Churn is found past a limestone pavement before returning directly to Alum Pot. Back at the stile the short-lived green lane is superseded at a gate/stile by a faint wallside track, swinging left at a wall corner towards Gill Garth Farm. Penyghent totally dominates all these parts. Though the track improves, leave it by going straight ahead to a ladder-stile. With a parallel wall just over to your left, keep on through two more fields to meet a grassy track bearing right to a gate just ahead at the foot of an extensive pasture. A broad green way sets forth up its gentle slope to its ultimate target of the far top corner. From a gate here a level track runs on to quickly arrive at the path crossroads at Sulber. Here the path ascending Ingleborough from Horton crosses the Selside–Austwick bridleway.

8. Go straight across on the continuing grass track, rising very gently to a gate/stile. Immediately through, leave by a small gate on your left, a spectacular moment revealing the magnificent bowl of Thieves Moss below. A little path drops left down onto this limestone plateau. With patches of heather to your left, an early cairn

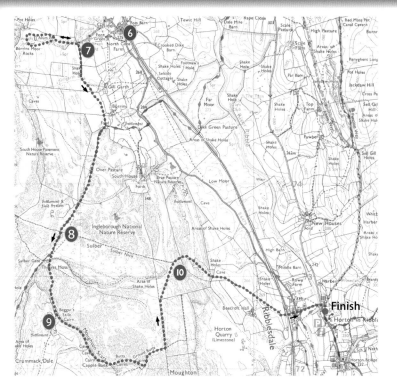

indicates the main path swinging right on the slightest of rises to run between the fractured pavements. Through a minor trough and curving round to the right, a grassier path continues as the limestone temporarily recedes. It returns and the path dips and rises slightly to the nick that looks down on Beggar's Stile.

9. Don't drop to the stile but rise very slightly left on a sketchy path, quickly levelling out and running intermittently along near the rim of the plateau pavement of Moughton Scars, with views down into Crummack Dale. Simply maintain this course high above the edge, ultimately looking down upon a colourful gulf through which a path rises out of the valley. Continue around the edge to meet it as it gains the crest. Now head away on this clear path onto a heathery plateau, swinging left to a ruinous shooting butt then bearing right to run past a series of them to a wall. Over the ladder-stile turn sharp left with the wall to a bridle-gate, then the path bears off right across level terrain to quickly meet the Sulber path at a dewpond.

10. Turning right this well-tramped path returns you unfailingly to Horton. Dropping down through a gateway it slants right down to a bridle-gate. It then meanders down and across rough pastures to a bridle-gate after which it dips across a farm road. Rising beyond it the path runs along to a little gate revealing the railway station just below. Drop down this final field to cross the line and down its access road into the village. Penyghent's masterful presence rounds things off nicely.

THE LIMESTONE COUNTRY AROUND CLAPHAM AND AUSTWICK IS AN ARCHETYPAL DALES LANDSCAPE, WITH GLEAMING WHITE SCARS AND PAVEMENTS. THE OBJECTIVE OF THIS WALK, HOWEVER, IS AN INTRIGUING AREA OF GEOLOGICAL INTRUDERS: THE NORBER BOULDERS WERE CARRIED TO THEIR PRESENT POSITION BY A RETREATING GLACIER FROM FURTHER UP CRUMMACK DALE. WHAT IS SO UNUSUAL IS THAT THEY ARE DARK SILURIAN ROCKS ATOP WHITE LIMESTONE PEDESTALS THAT HAVE WORN MORE RAPIDLY AWAY. THEY ARE TERMED 'ERRATIC', AND ARE A BIT SPECIAL.

Clapham is a lovely village at the base of mighty Ingleborough, from where Clapham Beck flows to form the centrepiece. Several attractive bridges are in evidence, and splendid cottages line the parallel lane. Centrally placed are the New Inn, shops and cafes. By the car park is the Manor House with a 1705 lintel, while just up the road is St James's Church with a 15th-century tower. For many decades Clapham provided the cottage home for that revered Yorkshire magazine *The Dalesman*. Alpine plants from far-flung parts were brought back to the grounds of Ingleborough Hall by botanist Reginald Farrer (1880–1920). At the start of the walk you pass beneath a pair of dark tunnels built by the Farrars for access from the hall to their grounds at the entrance to Clapdale. Higher up Clapdale is Ingleborough Cave, with guided tours.

Austwick is an attractive village with a small green, the cosy Gamecock Inn and countless tidy cottages. The tiny church of the Epiphany with its little bell-cote sits at the green junction, as does a shop. Across the fields, Feizor is an unspoilt settlement at the terminus for motor vehicles of a short cul-de-sac to this hollow in the hills. Footpaths, however, radiate in all directions. A little beyond its splendid cafe is a lovely corner with a water pump and trough sat on a tiny green outside a row of cottages.

At 1,191ft/363m the colourful top of Smearsett Scar marks the walk's highest point. Its character is rivalled by its status as a viewpoint, and it is probably the finest spot for appraising the newly revealed Ribblesdale landscape. Included are Horton and Helwith Bridge backed by Plover Hill, Penyghent and Fountains Fell; then come Stainforth, its Scar, and Settle's inimitable hills. Pot Scar forms an enticing objective along the undulating escarpment to the west.

THE BASICS

Distance: 9½ miles / 15.25km

Gradient: Several short, steeper pulls

Severity: Moderate

Approx. time to walk: 5 to 6 hours

Stiles: Twenty-six

Maps: OS Landranger 98 Wensleydale & Upper Wharfedale; Explorer OL2 Yorkshire Dales South/West and Explorer OL41 Forest of Bowland

Path description: Mostly firm tracks and field paths

Start Point: Clapham village centre (GR SD 745692)

Parking: National Park car park (LA2 8HH)

Dog friendly: Sheep pastures, so dogs on leads please, they should be fit and able to manage stiles

Public toilets: At start

Nearest food: Pub and cafe at start, pub at Austwick, cafe at Feizor

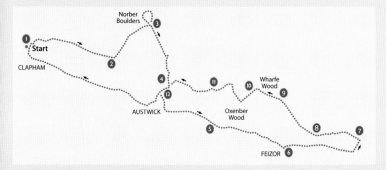

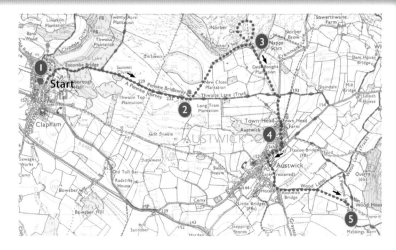

The Route

1. From the car park rejoin its access road by Clapham Beck, and turn right past cottages and the entrance to Ingleborough Hall. Arriving at the church, bear right outside the churchyard wall, as a bridleway takes over to pass beneath a couple of long, dark tunnels. An initially steep climb through woodland levels out just short of the junction of Thwaite Lane and Long Lane. Keep straight on for some time, initially slightly rising, with Ingleborough appearing back over to the left.

2. After a slight drop take a stile/gate on the left, from where a faint path crosses to the right of the marshy site of a tarn. Ahead is the imposing cliff of Robin Proctor's Scar, while around you are scattered Silurian boulders. Keep right to a wall corner, following it along to a stile beneath the scar. In open country advance on with the wall on your right to reach a fork; the one dropping with the wall is your onward route, but for now rise left to

a guidepost at a path crossroads on a little shelf amid scattered Silurian rocks: you are now just beneath the Norber boulderfield. Turn left, squeezing up between limestone outcrops to a prominent large cairn on a pile of stones. You are now on the plateau on which the boulders rest, largely along to the right. Explore!

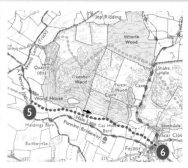

3. Back at the guidepost drop onto the lower path, which traces the wall down to a stile by a small gate at the bottom. Head away with the wall on your right, and part way along bear left to a gate near the corner. Rejoining Thwaite Lane, go left a few steps to a crossroads with Crummack Lane, and turn right to descend into Austwick via Town Head. At the bottom turn right into the centre, soon reaching the Gamecock Inn.

4. From the green outside the pub turn down the narrow lane opposite, and quickly take a snicket on the right. Past the houses it emerges as a flagged path running through two fields to emerge onto the road on the edge of the village. Turn left to cross Austwick Bridge. Immediately over, turn left along the walled track of Wood Lane. Where it bends left, leave by a gate/stile on the right to cross the length of a field to a stile onto a walled bridleway to the right of Wood House. Turning right would provide a stile-free route into Feizor. Preferably cross straight over the bridleway to climb the field opposite to a stile on the brow. Pause here to appraise the fine view.

5. From the stile begin a generally obvious march through a string of stiles in this tidy block of fields with Oxenber and Feizor Woods on the left. The stiles come thick and fast towards the end, maintaining a near-straight line to emerge into Feizor across a tiny beck.

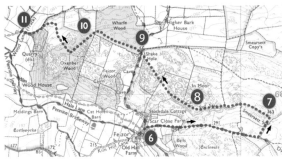

6. Go briefly left towards the cafe, and leave by a stile on the right. Across a small enclosure you pass through a barnyard into a field. Ascend with the wall on your right to a stile near the top. High to your left rises the gleaming vertical wall of Pot Scar. Entering Open Access land, a super path continues the ascent through more colourful country, and its groove fades to reveal Smearsett Scar ahead. Advance on through an old wall junction on the brow to a stile in a sturdy wall. Through another old wall the path crosses the edge of the upland hollow to approach a stile ahead. Before it, however, take a wallside path running left to a stile in a kink directly beneath Smearsett Scar. A thin path ascends the wallside to its brow, from where you strike left up through the edge of the outcrops to quickly attain the summit.

7. Leave by heading west on an intermittent trod along the edge of the escarpment, bound for Pot Scar: part way on, a scar deflects you 'inland'. Drop down a gap in the scarp and cross to the old wall, then rise on intermittent paths to the unmistakable crown of Pot Scar. At 1,148ft/350m a massive pile of stones is surmounted by a circular shelter. Just a short way beneath is the rim of the sheer limestone walls.

8. A trod drops down to a stile in the wall just ahead, and runs on above further cliffs. It veers away from the declining edge, down to the start of a long, curving scar. Negotiate this and as the trod fades, bear right to meet the wall ahead; almost at

once you encounter a sturdy stile built into it. This reveals further lovely terrain of scattered trees and stony outcrops. From the stile bear right towards the wall corner then cross to a path, going left on it to a gate/stile onto the rough road through Feizor Nick.

9. Turn right on it through a gate, but within a few paces go left to a stile into Wharfe Wood where a couple of waymarked trails have been created. A path heads away on a meandering course through scattered scrubby trees, soon swinging left up to a clearing on a knoll. Here it bears right to almost merge with a wall on the left. The path gently declines into denser trees to arrive at a wall-stile in a corner. This puts you into Oxenber Wood.

10. The path drops into more open surrounds. Soon swinging left it rises gently to run through largely open terrain amid scattered limestone. Soon entering a vast, flat clearing, a junction of the two main paths is reached. Double back right, soon descending colourful open pasture. Swinging right to drop down towards a clump of trees, the path then swings left beneath it and grandly down through bracken to a path and intake wall along the base. Go left on this through a gate/stile, and the green path drops down with the wall to a gate/stile at the bottom. A short-lived walled path drops down onto another walled way, Wood Lane again.

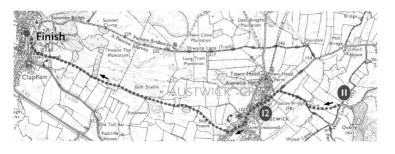

11. Just a few paces left take a stile on the right, and descend the field to find a stile at the very bottom. This puts you onto a walled bridleway. Turn right to a ford at Flascoe Bridge, an old clapper bridge on Austwick Beck. Across, the way soon broadens out and runs on to the road on the edge of Austwick. Turn left back into the village.

12. Continue past the pub to the green outside the shop, and keep right on the Clapham road until reaching a gate on the right between houses. Accessing a field corner a grassy way slants left up the field, crossing to a stile in the far wall and along to another. The path rises slightly above a small wood to maintain a simple line through the fields, the latter stages seeing old iron kissing gates replacing the stiles. Latterly a fence accompanies you along to meet the right-angle of a farm track. The path runs a parallel course to its right, later briefly entering the edge of the farmyard, and at the end running enclosed again to the car park.

Lovely Dentdale is one of the quieter corners of the Dales. Its river, the Dee, runs an enviable course from high fells in the centre of the National Park, carving its way down to run more calmly through iconic sheep pastures shared by countless small farms, to meet the River Rawthey on the edge of Sedbergh. The valley remains enviably enshrouded in a near timeless quality, and forms a perfect cushion between the Three Peaks and the Howgill Fells.

Dent is only a village in size, but is still known as Dent Town in recognition of a once greater importance. Today it is an unhurried backwater midway along its own valley; the only roads in and out are minor ones, a factor which has helped preserve Dent's character. Retained are some cobbled streets lined with neat cottages, cafes and a pair of pubs. St Andrew's church dates in part from the 15th century; the tower dates from the late 18th century. Between the Sun Inn and the George and Dragon is a block of Shap granite serving as a drinking fountain, and carved with the name Adam Sedgwick. Born here in 1785, he spent over 50 years as Professor of Geology at Cambridge, and did much research into the fascinating geology of his own back yard.

At least one of the village pubs serves ale brewed just up the road in this very dale: support a local industry and savour an excellent product at the same time! Also here are a Methodist church built as a Wesleyan Chapel in 1834, and a Zion Chapel of 1835 that now serves as a meditation centre. A heritage centre gives an excellent picture of the area in times past, while the National School of 1845 still serves the dale's youngsters.

Directly behind the village, Flinter Gill tumbles over a series of rock ledges in a deep, wooded ravine, though after a dry spell the beck may be conspicuous by its absence. It leads you steeply uphill to meet the Occupation Road. Running across the northern flank of Great Coum, it links the Dent–Ingleton road with that from Dent to Barbon. An old packhorse way and service road for the enclosures, it provides marvellous sweeping views over the dale.

The walk along the Dee's banks is mercurial, no more so than in springtime when the lush fields are full of new-born lambs. The crystal-clear Dee is in sedate mood, and much of your walk is overlooked by the colourful hollow of Combe Scar on the south side and the more docile Rise Hill to the north.

THE BASICS

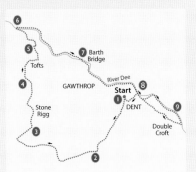

Distance: 8½ miles / 13.5km

Gradient: One sustained climb for the first mile

Severity: Moderate

Approx. time to walk: 4½ to 5 hours

Stiles: Thirteen

Maps: OS Landranger 98 Wensleydale & Upper Wharfedale; Explorer OL2 Yorkshire Dales South/West

Path description: Mostly firm tracks and riverbank paths

Start Point: Dent village centre (GR SD 704870)

Parking: Village car park (LA10 5QP)

Dog friendly: Sheep pastures, so dogs on leads please, they should be fit and able to manage stiles

Public toilets: At start

Nearest food: Pubs and cafes at start

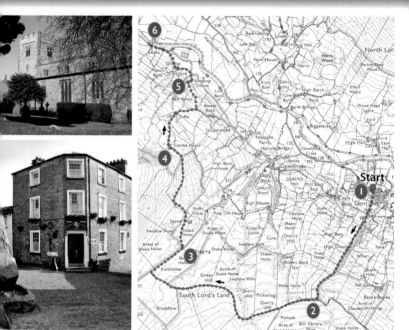

The Route

1. From the car park cross the road and take the one rising away past the school. A delightful group of cottages precedes the start of Flinter Gill. At the last cottage the stony track of Flintergill Outrake takes over to climb above the beck. Features of interest punctuate what is a steep and stony climb. Immediately on the left are the Dancing Slabs, a flat shelf of rock used by local weavers for dampening and trampling on their cloth to improve it! This is followed by the Wishing Tree. Higher, a gate on the right gives access to High Ground Farmstead, a barn containing a small museum of farming implements. Back on route you pass a restored limekiln with a small quarry behind. Near the top of Flinter Gill the way emerges from its wooded confines and the gradients finally ease out. A stile on the right just before a gate gives access to a modern toposcope which details the magnificent view of Dentdale leading down to the Howgill Fells. Largely enclosed by walls but easier underfoot, the way rises to quickly join an enclosed track, the Occupation Road.

2. Turn right along the Occupation Road's wide course for a long, elevated stride. Soon reaching a high point at around 1,180ft/360m, the way gradually curves around and down to eventually meet the Dent–Barbon road. Accompany the road briefly right, rising gently to its summit at around 985ft/300m on Stone Rigg. Looking back, Great Coum forms a long, flat skyline.

3. From a gate on the left a grassy track heads diagonally away, keeping left of profuse limestone outcrops to a ladder-stile in the far corner. From it a rougher

track heads left with an old wall towards the steep slope, and while a quad track scales the slope, a firmer track swings right across a scrubby bank. This superb promenade gives massive views up the dale, featuring Dent itself: Baugh Fell looms over the shoulder of Rise Hill ahead. From a gate at the end the super green way continues, enclosed, to Combe House. This shelters beneath the striking hollow of Combe Scar, a colourful scene chiselled out of the northern flank of Middleton Fell: a popular Dentdale landmark, its low crags give it more then a hint of Lakeland.

4. Follow the rough drive dropping away, and as it winds down through old walls, forsake it for a path making a bee-line for the buildings at Tofts. A tiny footbridge on a tree-lined beck precedes steps up the opposite bank. Through a small gate pass between the buildings and out on the drive, to be rejoined by Combe House drive. The track drops gradually down towards the farmhouse at Bower Bank, but before reaching it, as the track levels out, locate a gate in the dip just down to your left. Bear left down the field, passing a ruin to find the start of a cart track just beyond it. This descends the next field to the bottom corner, where, dropping left, a gate puts you into the yard at Raw Bank.

5. Go right the few strides onto a back road. Turn briefly left, and as the road drops away, go straight ahead along the short access road to Dillicar. Head straight on through the yard, bearing left at the end (with the house to your left) and dropping down a track out into a field. Slant down to the right to a ladder-stile back onto the back road. Go left on it the short way to a footbridge and ford by the cottage at Ellers.

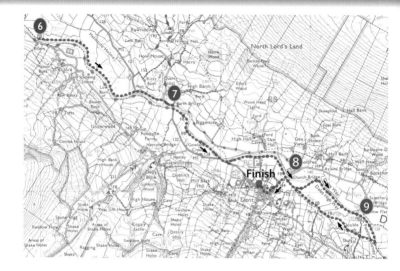

6. Cross the bridge and set off back along the other bank, this lengthy section being on a flood embankment clinging by the river along Helmside Holme. At the end a wooded bank forces you up onto the road opposite a monument honouring Lucy Elam, who in 1876 footed the bill for a re-routing of this section of road.

7. Being wary of traffic on this bend, turn right to quickly arrive at Barth Bridge. Cross and take a flight of steps on the left, down into a field. Virtually at once you pass near a spring emerging from the riverbank. Cross straight over through a couple of fields to a kissing gate, and across to meet the riverbank again. Now turn right for a lovely stroll upstream, passing through several kissing gates until one puts you briefly onto a road. Almost at once you are returned to the riverbank. Various stiles and gates are encountered before the path becomes partially enclosed to hug the river more tightly along to stone steps up onto Church Bridge.

8. Unless wanting to finish now, cross the road onto a path opposite. Resuming upstream, you are immediately deflected from the Dee by Keld Beck. Follow this just as far as a farm bridge on it, across which cross to a wall just ahead and then bear right with this as it guides a path curving back to the river. Simply head upstream on a largely enclosed path that faithfully shadows the enchanting Dee. Keep straight on the riverbank at a junction with a bridleway at a ford and stepping

stones. Ahead, mighty Whernside encloses Deepdale. Two minutes beyond the ford is a major confluence with Deepdale Beck. This lovely spot deserves a pause: the side beck can often be entirely dry here.

9. Deepdale Beck – or at least its deep course – is now briefly traced, but only for a minute as far as reaching a wall and hand-gate, with the house at Double Croft across to the right. Turn right along the near side of the wall to a gate by a barn at the end onto the enclosed cart track of Double Croft Lane opposite the idyllically sited house. Without entering the grounds, take a stile straight in front, then cross to a stile beyond it and advance on a briefly enclosed green way. Through a gate at the end continue on with a hedge on your left, and keep on to a stile at the very end. From here a clear path shadows a tiny beck through scrub, leaving by a stile just before the end. In front a gate/stile point to a ford and stepping-stones on the larger Keld Beck just above, but your way takes the adjacent stile and crosses to one in the corner just beyond. Here a good enclosed path shadows Keld Beck back to the farm bridge from earlier. Cross it and retrace steps back to Church Bridge, just ahead, then turn left up the road back into the centre.

THIS DELIGHTFUL RAMBLE IN THE NORTH-WESTERN CORNER OF THE DALES IS DOMINATED BY THE LUSH BANKS OF THE RIVER RAWTHEY, WHICH IN TURN IS DOMINATED BY THE HOWGILL FELLS WHICH RISE ABOVE THE LITTLE MARKET TOWN OF SEDBERGH. A VISIT TO A HISTORIC QUAKER ESTABLISHMENT ADDS FURTHER INTEREST.

Sedbergh is the largest settlement in the Yorkshire Dales National Park, yet its isolation has helped it avoid commercialism. Becoming part of Cumbria in 1974, Sedbergh – omit the last two letters in pronunciation – boasts an unparalleled position on the lower slopes of its very own Howgill Fells. In the neighbourhood of Sedbergh three lively rivers end their journeys as the Dee, Clough and Rawthey join forces to swell the waters of the River Lune. Aside from the imposing fells, Sedbergh is dominated by its public school, founded in the early 16th century. Old boys include Adam Sedgwick the geologist, while the best known in more recent times is former England rugby caption Will Carling. Most other features will be found on or near the lengthy main street, including the lovely St Andrew's Church, with a 15th-century tower and other parts dating back to Norman times.

In the beautiful setting of the former weaving hamlet of Brigflatts is a historic Friends' Meeting House. Incorporating a 1675 date stone, it is one of the oldest Quaker establishments in the country, and still put to its original use. Its atmospheric interior is regularly open to view, and is worth a few respectful minutes of anyone's time. The attractive house of High Brigflatts, opposite, bears a 1743 date stone, while at the point where you enter the hamlet is a Quaker burial ground.

The height of the Railway Age saw lines built through extraordinarily remote places, and the former Clapham–Lowgill branch was a spectacular example as it traced the Lune Valley beneath the western limit of the Dales. It is met twice on this walk, both 'over and under' as it approached Sedbergh's station.

Winder is Sedbergh's patron fell, a shapely knoll whose ascent is a 'must' when around Sedbergh. Its superb panorama includes a fine prospect up to the Lune Gorge and less frequented western Howgills. Garsdale and Dentdale are particularly appealing as they burrow deep into the higher fells of the Dales. Drop a little towards Sedbergh for an intimate bird's-eye picture, a fitting scene as Winder is the town's 'special' fell.

THE BASICS

Distance: 8 miles / 12.75km

Gradient: Sustained but easy climb onto Winder

Severity: Quite strenuous

Approx. time to walk: 4 to 5 hours

Stiles: Thirteen

Maps: OS Landranger 97 Kendal & Morecambe and 98 Wensleydale & Upper Wharfedale; Explorer OL19 Howgill Fells & Upper Eden Valley

Path description: Riverbank and field paths followed by grassy paths on open fell

Start Point: Sedbergh town centre (GR SD 658921)

Parking: Two central car parks (LA10 5AD)

Dog friendly: Sheep pastures, so dogs on leads please, they should be fit and able to manage stiles

Public toilets: At start

Nearest food: Pubs and cafes at start

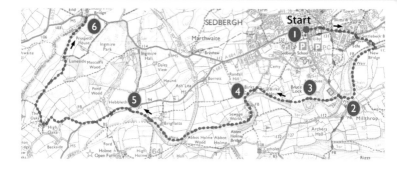

The Route

1. Head east out to the edge of town and turn right down the Hawes road. Immediately after crossing New Bridge take steps on the right down to a path which runs downstream with the River Rawthey. Remaining close by the river through open surrounds, it passes a weir and curves pleasantly around to a small gate onto a road at Millthrop Bridge.

2. Cross the bridge and take a small iron gate after a drive on the left. Bear right across the field to a stile into a wood at the end. Remain on the left-hand path above a steep drop to the Rawthey. Soon reaching another fork, the right branch leads through an intriguing walled sunken section. Soon emerging, take the right-hand of two paths heading left, quickly leaving the wood at a kissing gate. Go left with the fence past the wood corner to a brow by the remains of a small folly. To the right, Winder fronts the ever-enticing prospect of the Howgills; you'll be standing on top of it before the walk is over!

3. Keep straight on down the field towards the Rawthey and head

downstream past a sports field. The path then rises towards a lone house, running left of it to join a narrow lane. Go left past cottages at Birks to reach Birks Mill in a grand riverside setting. This cotton-spinning mill now has a more modern use; note also the former mill-race immediately downstream.

4. Ignoring the footbridge, take a path downstream by the rear yard, initially squeezed between the Rawthey and a treatment works. The path clings to the riverbank all the way to Brigflatts Farm. En route you quickly pass a delightful confluence with the River Dee. The route is then interrupted by the former branch railway alongside a tall, single-arched iron river bridge; its embankment must be scaled to descend the other side. Approaching Brigflatts the path becomes tightly enclosed, climbing past the rear of the farm (with a glimpse of the white-walled Friends' Meeting House) to run above a wooded bank of the river to a kissing gate onto the A683 Sedbergh–Kirkby Lonsdale road. With no direct access to Brigflatts from the riverbank, to make a visit you must double back along the road to its beautiful setting in the old weaving hamlet of Brigflatts.

5. Back on the road, go left for a few cautious minutes then look out for a kissing gate hidden on the right. Follow the fence away to cross a tiny stream, then rise half-left over a knoll to cross to the far corner, a hedgerowed green way running left to reach High Oaks. The principal house in this attractive hamlet bears a 1706 date stone. Turn right after the main house, then right again to leave by a pleasant hedged track. From a stile at its demise, keep right to a gate at the very far end. A splendid grassy track leads to Luneside Farm, becoming enclosed in the process. After the buildings, leave its drive by a gate on the left, then cross to a fence on the left and follow it away to a stile. Now slant down to trace the River Lune upstream to the A684 Kendal–Sedbergh road at Lincoln's Inn Bridge. The unevenly arched bridge recalls a hostelry on its other side; only a farm remains.

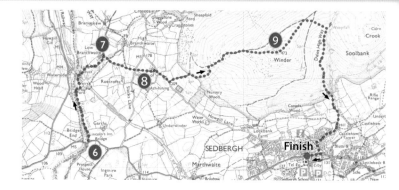

6. Cross the road, not the bridge, and go right a few strides to a gate to resume this happy interlude with the Lune. Along the charming riverbank the Lune Viaduct soon appears ahead, preceded by a footbridge on Crosdale Beck. The red sandstone and metal arches loom dramatically  above a pastoral scene. The way passes under the tall arches before slanting uphill. On fading, cross to find a corner stile opposite, from where a fieldside track heads away with the parallel beck to Low Branthwaite.

7. Don't rise to the house but turn right down its access road. Immediately after bridging a small stream take a stile on the right, and rise to another by a gate just above. Now bear right across the field and up the far side to a small gate part way

up, then continue steeply up past a modern barn on your left to find a stile at the top onto a narrow road. Cross straight over to another stile and ascend towards the glimpse of a house at Height of Winder that is visible. From a kissing gate in the top corner advance on the short way to a stile just past the house, then left across a paddock in front of it to a wall-stile onto its drive.

8. Go right the few strides to the road, and turn right briefly uphill. On the viewpoint brow, turn left up a walled grassy way climbing to a gate onto the open fell on the base of Winder. The track rises right, briefly with the wall to a brow, then swings away left to start the ascent of Winder's colourful flanks. All you need to do is follow this superb, well-graded grassy track up the spur, and before too long you will gain Winder's summit. At 1,551ft/473m it is crowned by an Ordnance Survey column and a topograph.

9. Leave by the broad path heading away north-east, declining very gently along the broad ridge aiming for the rounded prow of the loftier Arant Haw. Dropping towards a dip, bear right on a thinner path contouring across to meet a broader ascending path. Cross straight over on your thinner continuation that drops down to meet a second broader path just short of the ravine of Settlebeck Gill. Turn right down this, a delightful descent above the gill with glorious views. When it forks lower down, either path will lead to seats and an old iron kissing gate at the foot of the fell, still overlooking the gill. A lovely enclosed path drops down above the wooded gill, then through a kissing gate for a short enclosed spell down to a stile into a field. Joining a track here drop down and along to the right, joining an access track to a gate out onto a road end. Simply follow this the short way down back onto the main street.

THE HOWGILL FELLS ARE A COMPACT, WELL-DEFINED UPLAND RANGE. TRIANGULAR IN SHAPE, THE GROUP IS MOATED BY THE RIVER LUNE ON TWO SIDES AND THE RIVER RAWTHEY ON THE OTHER. THE FELLS ARE NAMED FROM THE MODEST SETTLEMENT FROM WHERE THIS WALK BEGINS.

This surprising naming – rather than the obvious choice of Sedbergh – only found its way onto maps in quite recent times. This alone may have helped keep the hills relatively undisturbed; certainly more people gasp at their splendour from 70mph on the M6 motorway than ever set foot on their inviting slopes. Along with The Calf, four further independent mountains rise above the 2,000ft/610m mark. Additionally there are several lesser 2,000ft tops and a whole array of lower summits spread along the radiating ridges and outer fringes. They are an absolute joy to explore.

Scattered along the western base of the fells, Howgill's peaceful farming community has at its modest focal point the little church of the Holy Trinity beside Chapel Beck, dating from 1838.

At 2,218ft/676m The Calf marks the summit of the Howgill Fells. The Calf's plateau, however, restricts its views to distant lines of the Cross Fell group in the North Pennines, and the widely spread hills of the Dales to east and south. On a clear day the serrated Lakeland skyline to the west will claim most attention beyond a Lune Valley foreground; Morecambe Bay is also well seen. A cairn stands across the main path from the OS column, with an often-dry pool beyond.

One of the lesser but still popular summits, at 1,985ft/605m Arant Haw enjoys grand views of the western cirque of high Howgills, from Fell Head around to Calders. More distantly, the long Lakeland skyline features Black Combe, the Coniston Fells, the Scafells and Great Gable, with the Helvellyn group over Ill Bell and High Street.

THE BASICS

Distance: 7½ miles / 12km

Gradient: A sustained but easy climb onto high fells

Severity: Strenuous

Approx. time to walk: 4 to 5 hours

Stiles: Three

Maps: OS Landranger 97 Kendal & Morecambe and 98 Wensleydale & Upper Wharfedale; Explorer OL19 Howgill Fells & Upper Eden Valley

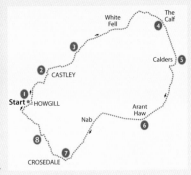

Path description: Mostly excellent grass paths on open fellsides

Start Point: Howgill Church, 2¾ miles on Howgill Lane out of Sedbergh (GR SD 633950). Start from a hollow behind a gated road

Parking: Thoughtful parking alongside the start point. A donation in the church collecting box would be a nice gesture for use of the verge (LA10 5JD)

Dog friendly: Sheep pastures and open fellside, so dogs on leads please, they should be fit and able to manage stiles

Public toilets: Nearest at Sedbergh

Nearest food: Nearest at Sedbergh

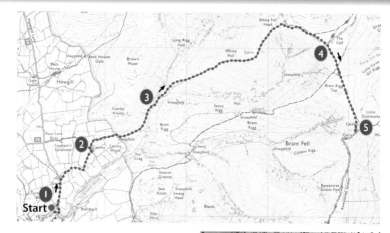

The Route

1. Rejoining Howgill Lane turn left over the bridge, and head steeply uphill to the farm at Gateside; already the day's skyline is evident to the right. From a stile on the right before the farm, head on to the end of the buildings then bear left to a corner gate. Just above, join a track bearing right and swinging in to fade as it bridges a tiny stream. Rise up the steep slope in front to find a stile in a wall at the top, then slant right beneath a small stand of trees to a small corner gate above. This reveals the full promise of your walk, with the high Howgills ridge ahead. Drop briefly with the wall on your left, and through a gate in it a track rises left to Castley Farm.

2. Ascend the driveway between the buildings to a track junction at the top. While the drive turns left your

way is right, the enclosed cart track rising again before levelling out for a grand stroll along to a gate onto the open fell. The track drops slightly right to head off towards the hills, slanting down above Long Rigg Beck to drop to a ford on it. A fantastic sense of remoteness pervades in this lovely spot.

3. The track fords the beck to commence the long and uncomplicated ascent of White Fell. Initially steep and rough, stay on the main track which improves to rise ever more delightfully up this broad spur. To your left is distinctive Fell Head, with Bram Rigg Top and Calders in front and Arant Haw over to the right; ironically it is only The Calf itself which remains hidden until much higher. Several grooved sections add to the delights, as do views back to a long skyline of the Lakeland Fells. Higher, the path slants right in a splendid groove, looking down on the deep upper reaches of Calf Beck. The Three Peaks appear far across to the right, while the gleaming white OS column of The Calf also appears – much nearer! As the going eases keep to the main right path above the steeper slopes falling right, contouring around and doubling back right to confirm its goal of The Calf. Passing beneath the minor highest point of White Fell Head, the path merges with the Fell Head–Calf path from the left for the final short pull to the waiting OS column.

4. Leave The Calf by bearing right on the firm Sedbergh path, dropping to a minor depression then rising onto the shoulder of Bram Rigg Top, whose minor summit at 2,204ft/672m is just across to the right. The main path continues south to very quickly reach the cairn on Calders. At 2,211ft/674m this superbly sited summit is a fine vantage point on the edge of a more pronounced drop than The Calf.

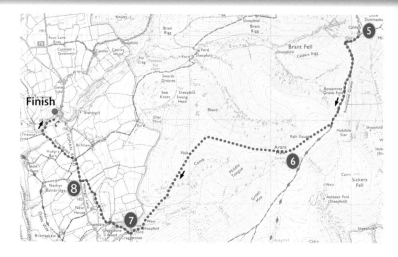

5. From the adjacent fence corner the broad path swings right, descending steeply to the saddle of Rowantree Grains. Improving underfoot as it goes, the fence is left behind to rise briefly to a shoulder of Arant Haw. Just short of the brow leave the main path for a much thinner one that bears gently right up and along to Arant Haw's summit cairn at 1,985ft/605m.

6. Leave Arant Haw by resuming westwards to commence the descent on a delightful little path down the gentle ridge. Reaching a saddle in front of a minor knoll the thin path forks. While the right branch surmounts the knoll, your way is the left one, briefly contouring before resuming the descent onto the south-westerly spur of Nab. The intermittent path crosses its top before beginning the steeper final section, now a thin but clear trod. Deflected left by a wall corner, a track is met

above Crosdale Beck. Before it passes through a corner gate off the fell, instead drop left to a ford on the stream by sheep pens. The stream crossing makes for a pleasant final linger, with aggressively rocky walls immediately downstream. A rough track slants up the other side, keeping right to very quickly find a gate off the fell.

7. Don't advance to the cottage at Craggstone, but head down the enclosure to a small gate into trees above the stream, noting a splendid waterfall. The thin path drops to a footbridge on Crosdale Beck then slants up to Crosdale Farm just above. Go left through the yard, but, level with the house on the left, pass through a small gate onto its drive. Head right on this, but within a few strides leave through another small gate ahead. Cross straight over an access track to a gate from where a farm track heads off with a hedge. It runs on through a second field to an odd arrangement of gate and stile at a stream crossing. After a briefly enclosed section, head away along the right side of the field, passing through a gate midway to resume on the other side of the wall. A gate at the end puts you onto an enclosed farm track; go left onto Howgill Lane.

8. Turn right as far as a crossroads with Birkhaw Drive, and, for a varied finish, take the meandering back road to the left. Up to the right, enjoy a fine picture of these western Howgills. Ignoring all branches left, the road winds round to drop down to Mill House. The former mill stands alongside; note the long-dry water cut that once supplied the waterwheel at the mill from Chapel Beck. The church, and thus the finish, also appears just ahead.

UPPER WENSLEYDALE IS HEMMED IN BY HIGH AND EXTENSIVE FELLS, BUT AT HAWES IT BROADENS OUT INTO AN ARRANGEMENT OF GREEN PASTURES WHERE SHEEP AND CATTLE GRAZE TO THEIR HEARTS' CONTENT. THOUGH NOT AS DRAMATIC AS SOME OF THE DALES, ITS SEDATE APPEARANCE HIDES A MYRIAD OLD VILLAGES AND IMPRESSIVE WATERFALLS, AS WELL AS A STRING OF SIDE VALLEYS ALONG ITS SOUTHERN FLANK.

Hawes is the 'capital' of Upper Wensleydale, and retains an unconventional layout well worth a leisurely exploration. This lively little market town gains even greater character at its Tuesday market, when there are, happily, as many locals in evidence as there are tourists. Once the last stop on the Wensleydale branch line, its former station is now the Dales Countryside Museum, with a National Park Centre alongside. Two surviving industries are today also tourist attractions. The ropemakers is also by the old station, where you can observe and purchase any number of associated products. The creamery, meanwhile, is a long-established business that has become a hugely popular visitor centre offering a 'must-do' experience. Milk from cows you might see on your walks is used in the production of the celebrated Wensleydale cheese: from watching the cows munch the grass to nibbling the finished product, you can enjoy the whole experience!

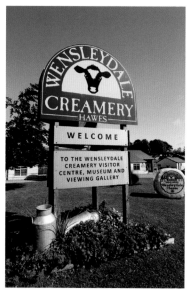

At the unspoiled hamlet of Sedbusk, farms and cottages look across the dale to Hawes and beyond from an altitude a little under 1,000 feet. It is so laid back it has even avoided the back road from Hardraw to Askrigg, being reached only by a narrow lane. Rising behind is the long scar of High

Clint, the lengthy promenade along which you can enjoy extensive panoramas over Upper Wensleydale's wide surround of 2,000ft fells.

Hardraw is a tiny hamlet made famous by its waterfall, claimed to be the highest single drop above ground in England. It also has its own little church, St Mary and St John, and a tearoom. Access to Hardraw Force is through the Green Dragon pub, where a charge is made to view the spectacle: it is but a short walk into the increasingly impressive amphitheatre. The cliff over which the water spills is Hardraw Scaur, or Scar. In the gorge below the force, century-old band contests have been revived and take place each September – the bandstand is passed on the way.

THE BASICS

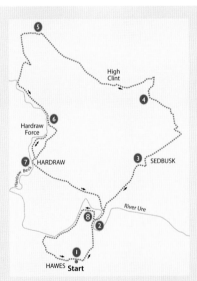

Distance: 7 miles / 11.25km

Gradient: Sustained uphill in opening stages

Severity: Quite strenuous

Approx. time to walk: 4 to 4½ hours

Stiles: Twenty

Maps: OS Landranger 98 Wensleydale & Upper Wharfedale; Explorer OL30 Yorkshire Dales North/Central

Path description: Good field paths, tracks and grassy paths on open fell

Start Point: Hawes town centre (GR SD 875898)

Parking: National Park car park (DL8 3NL)

Dog friendly: Sheep pastures, so dogs on leads please, they should be fit and able to manage stiles

Public toilets: At start

Nearest food: Pubs and cafes at start; pub and tearoom at Hardraw

The Route

1. Between the old railway bridge and the WCs leave the car park on a path slanting up onto the road. Turn right to follow it over the bridge and out of town on a footway. Within a minute an access road goes left, and at this point a kissing gate signals the route of the Pennine Way, whose flagged course is followed to rejoin the road at another kissing gate a little further on. Cross Haylands Bridge over the River Ure.

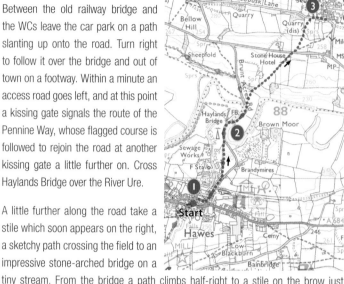

2. A little further along the road take a stile which soon appears on the right, a sketchy path crossing the field to an impressive stone-arched bridge on a tiny stream. From the bridge a path climbs half-right to a stile on the brow just above, from where a comprehensively flagged path ascends a large field to a stile in the top corner. Cross the road to a stile opposite, and resume the rise in the same direction to a stile ahead. Dropping to a stile just below, a steep climb goes past a barn leading to another stile in the top-right corner. Here you emerge onto narrow Sedbusk Lane: turn right to Sedbusk. At a junction by a Victorian postbox turn left to enter its confines, noting the former Primitive Methodist Chapel of 1875.

3. At the top end of the green bear right as the enclosed track of Shutt Lane takes over to climb away, with superb views across the valley. Immediately before a gate where it starts to run free, take a gate on the left from where a sunken way slants up a field. When this turns off, a path continues up to a tiny plantation, above which it slants left to a gate in a wall. The path then runs to a gate onto open fell; up to the right is an old limekiln.

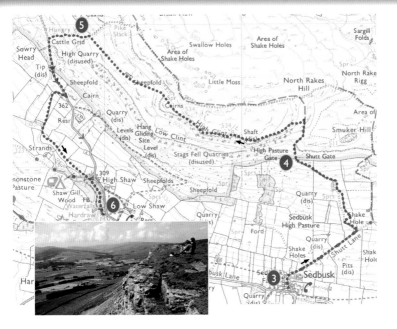

4. Continue up the track left of a low scar, but quickly break off to ascend easy slopes at the eastern end of High Clint above. Now head left for a superb ramble on faint ways atop the craggy scarp. Up to your right, Lovely Seat sits way back but is not a great deal higher. After almost a mile a prominent cairn to the right at 1,752ft/534m overlooks a splendid pair of stone men. As the scarp has now largely abated ignore its lesser, higher continuation ahead, and instead advance straight on from the beacons, descending tussocky ground in line with a large stone sheepfold ahead. Drop onto a grass track on this lower shelf, and go right beneath the folds: on your left is the more modest Low Clint. Remain on this edge until it fully fades, then slant gently down to a cattle grid visible on the Buttertubs road above Sowry Head.

5. Turn down over the grid and descend as far as a gate/stile at a parking verge on the right, where a grass track doubles back to a barn. From a gate/stile behind it descend the wallside to a stile at the bottom corner. A path drops down a wooded bank at a bend of Fossdale Gill, and out at the bottom it runs briefly with the beck. From a stile on the left leave it and cross several fields via gates and/ or stiles, in a straight line to approach High Shaw. Don't enter the yard: instead a little path deflects you right to steps down onto an access road. Turn right down this as far as a caravan site entrance, then take a small gate on the left into wooded Fossdale Gill. After seeing the waterfall a short way up, a flagged path accompanies the beck downstream. An early footbridge offers a choice of banks, and below two low falls a second footbridge is reached. Here leave the beck to prepare itself for its big moment, to be witnessed from below; a tall-walled path rises left to the road.

6. Go briefly right, and with Simonstone Hall (with a public bar) in front, take a drive on the right. Over a cattle grid/stile to a brow, it drops through two fields to West House Farm. Between the buildings advance to a stile, then go left a few strides to reveal Hardraw immediately below. Drop to a stile by a covered reservoir, then a solid path descends a steep field. Conclude through a small enclosure and a house yard to emerge onto the street alongside the pub.

7. To visit Hardraw Force, a fee must be paid at the pub, from where a well-made path joins Hardraw Beck to lead upstream past a bandstand to quickly reach an abrupt terminus beneath the waterfall. Back on the road, opposite the pub take a track left of the bridge to a kissing gate set back, from where an initially flagged path sets off to the left through the fields, linked by stiles. On losing its flags at a gateway keep straight on to a kissing gate at the end, then advance along the bottom edge of two fields to a small gate onto a road. Turn right, dropping down to pick up the outward route, and going right to re-cross Haylands Bridge.

8. Over the bridge immediately take a gate on the right and cross to a footbridge on the sizeable Gayle Beck. With the River Ure just ahead, instead bear left across the field, closing in on the wall to your left. At the end pass through a bridle-gate in it and a few stone flags put you onto the Ure's bank. A good path now follows this upstream, initially on a low embankment. After several more bridle-gates a brief

enclosed section is met. Emerging, the now invisible path forks. Bear left across the field to an old railway underpass, then bear left up the next field to cross to a stile in the wall ahead, well left of a gate. Cross to another straight ahead, then bear left to a small gate in a corner. Entering a yard, go left and then quickly right on the short access road out onto the main street in the centre of Hawes.

BAINBRIDGE IS A LOVELY WENSLEYDALE VILLAGE AROUND AN ENORMOUS GREEN FEATURING STOCKS AND THE HISTORIC ROSE AND CROWN. THE SITE OF THE ROMAN FORT OF VIROSIDUM OVERLOOKS THE VILLAGE TO THE EAST, WHILE THE NORMAN LORDS BASED THEIR FORESTERS HERE WHEN THE FOREST OF WENSLEYDALE WAS A POPULAR HUNTING GROUND. AT THE INN IS A HORN, BLOWN DURING THE WINTER MONTHS AT 9PM TO GUIDE BENIGHTED TRAVELLERS, ORIGINATING AS A WARNING SOUND IN THE DAYS OF THE FOREST.

Joining the Ure at Bainbridge is the very short-lived River Bain, the outflow from Semerwater. Your walk follows its course up to the lake, and you also cross its only two bridges. That at Bainbridge overlooks some fine waterfalls immediately upstream, while Semerwater Bridge looks out onto the lake itself.

Of Wensleydale's many side valleys, Raydale is special in that it contains a natural lake, a rare feature indeed for Yorkshire. Semerwater was the largest lake in the old North Riding, and has become a popular venue for peaceful watersports. At the lakefoot is the mighty Carlow Stone, said to have been dropped by a giant. Local legend also relates how a visitor who received an unfriendly welcome caused a whole 'city' to be submerged under the waters, leaving just one poor but hospitable couple safe. What is more certain is that Iron Age lake-dwellings existed here. Above the lake, between Marsett and Stalling Busk, Raydale proper is formed by merging with the lesser valleys of Bardale and Cragdale.

Stalling Busk is a peaceful farming settlement enjoying views of the lake from its hillside perch, while nearby Raydale Preserves has refreshments. Standing in isolation some 200 feet below the hamlet is the old church. Originally dating from 1603, it was rebuilt in 1722 and abandoned in 1909. The ruins romantically overlook the lake, and exude an atmosphere not felt at the replacement St Matthew's up by the houses.

Cam High Road is the Roman road running from Ribblehead to Bainbridge. On this walk you tread the easternmost section which points unerringly at Bainbridge. Even in this lower stretch the views are very good: an unrivalled length of Wensleydale can be seen, including Hawes, Askrigg and various individual features.

THE BASICS

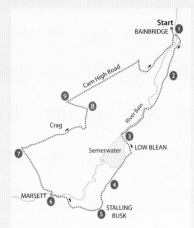

Distance: 9½ miles / 15.25km

Gradient: Two appreciable climbs

Severity: Strenuous

Approx. time to walk: 5 to 6 hours

Stiles: Twenty-two

Maps: OS Landranger 98 Wensleydale & Upper Wharfedale; Explorer OL30 Yorkshire Dales North/Central

Path description: Good field paths and tracks

Start Point: Bainbridge village centre (GR SD 933901)

Parking: Ample parking alongside the greens (DL8 3EL)

Dog friendly: Sheep pastures, so dogs on leads please, they should be fit and able to manage stiles

Public toilets: At start

Nearest food: Pub and tearoom at start

The Route

1. Leave Bainbridge by the main road to Aysgarth at the corner of the green, crossing the bridge over the River Bain and climbing the steep hill. Take a slim stile on the right just before a junction and head up the pasture; stay close by the wall on your left, well above the steep drop to the river. After a steep pull veer away from the wall, still rising to pass left of and above an 'island' field before levelling out. The first glimpse of Semerwater appears ahead. Along a brow the path runs to the right-hand of adjacent stiles.

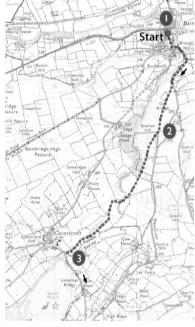

2. With Semerwater now fully in view a faint path heads away, diverging from the wall on your left to run closer to the edge of the steeper drop towards the river. It fades as you commence a gentle decline above the steeper bank. Dropping to a corner stile ahead just beyond a wall corner, advance on through stiles linking a couple of smaller fields to drop down a larger pasture to a gate/stile defended by moist terrain. Here go right to finally join the now adjacent River Bain. Its pleasant course offers a simple walk upstream to emerge onto a road at Semerwater Bridge, with the foot of Semerwater directly in front.

3. From the foreshore head left along the road away from the bridge, and at Low Blean Farm at the foot of the hill take a gate/stile on the right. Maintain a level course through the fields, taking in several stiles to one by a barn. A good path now drops down toward the lakeshore, though at an early stile it quickly angles away from it again. From a step-stile a good path slants gradually upwards across the rough pastures of Yorkshire Wildlife Trust's Semerwater reserve above the

head of the lake. From a stile at an information panel, slant up around a wall corner enclosing trees and along a wallside through a gate/ stile to arrive above the remains of Stalling Busk's old church. A stile accesses the ruin.

4.   Just beyond the church pass through a gate/stile, where the path forks. Go left on an improving path rising by a small, tree-lined stream; this old churchgoers' way rises to a gate at the top, then up a fieldside to a gate/stile on the edge of Stalling Busk. Continue on the short-lived farm track to a junction at a hairpin bend, where a slim path ascends open ground to emerge onto the cul-de-sac road in the hamlet.

5.   Go right just as far as the church, and at the sharp bend take the rough, enclosed track of Busk Lane down to the right. Though this enclosed way can be followed all the way down to a ford on Cragdale Water, a nicer option awaits. Vacate the lane part way down at a stile on the right just beyond gates either side, and head down the steep pasture. At the bottom continue close by the right-hand wall, crossing it at a stile towards the end to follow its other side to a stile at the very end. Behind it is a footbridge on Cragdale Water to rejoin your old way, now a stony track. Bear right on this, quickly crossing larger Raydale Beck at a ford/footbridge, a little beyond which it becomes enclosed by walls. The going improves as Marsett Beck is joined to lead to the hamlet, bearing right across its green to the road.

6. Cross the green to the road bridge, and turn right over it. Ignoring an access road left, advance a little further and double back left on an enclosed rough lane. Shortly after it starts to rise take a gate in the fence on the right and follow the wall away, rising to a wall-stile across the top. Resume on an improving green path, veering right of a tiny stream and the wall, and ascending more steeply through Marsett Cow Pasture. Easing out it passes through a fence-gate, with a pocket wood up to the right. Another steeper pull leads to a ladder-stile over the intake wall onto open fell, and an inviting path ascends steeply again. Addlebrough is magnificent beyond the lake. Gradually the path eases out, crossing a green track and along to a path crossroads at an old gateway. Big views ahead reveal a mountainous moorland skyline around Wensleydale.

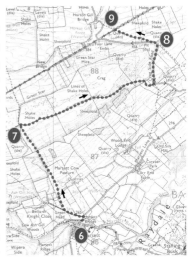

7. Turn right and follow the path close by the crest. Addlebrough returns to view; don't worry about the lake, as that will soon return in style. The path runs on through a gate then gains the true skyline to reach a distinctive limestone-capped knoll. At around 1,666ft/508m this is the walk's summit, with views north to Great Shunner Fell and Lovely Seat. Just past it another gate brings the lake dramatically into the scene. Here the path departs the ridge by slanting right, passing beneath a limestone scar and slanting mercurially down the flank above a small wood. At the bottom pass through a gate by sheep pens and cross right to the next gate, the green track then winding down and left to a gate onto Crag Side Road. Turn left, rising steadily to a bend at its highest point on Hawes End.

8. Go left for a couple of minutes further to a stile on the right, from where a thin path slants away gently left. Crossing a collapsed wall maintain this steady slant down the expansive reedy pasture to a stile onto a walled rough lane, Cam High Road. This section is classified as a byway, so you may encounter motorised vehicles exercising their legal rights.

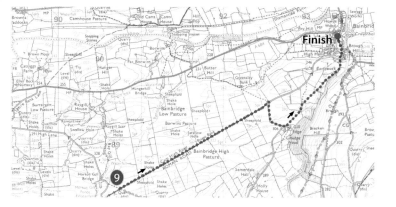

9. Turn right to follow the arrow-like course of the Roman road – which is in good condition for its age – until its eventual hijack by a modern road. Head up this as far as Gill Edge, just ahead, and turn left along its drive. This is home to the Wensleydale Equestrian Centre.

10. Before reaching the houses take a kissing gate on the left, and slant right down to a bridle-gate into a newly tree-planted area. Across the tiny stream rise to a stile in the wall, and head directly away to a stile. Now slant down to the right to pass through an old wall and on to the right of a barn. Bear right of a solid wall to a narrow gateway in the corner beyond, with the deep gill of the Bain just below. Contour on above the trees, converging to a stile at the end. Bainbridge is just below now; drop left down the steeper slope, through an old gateway and down to a small gate onto a drive, heading out to re-emerge onto the green.

ASKRIGG IS A WONDERFULLY DIFFERENT VILLAGE: FORMERLY A MARKET TOWN AND A FAMOUS CLOCK-MAKING CENTRE, ITS 1830 MARKET CROSS AND THREE-STOREY HOUSES RECALL BUSIER DAYS. THE 15TH-CENTURY ST OSWALD'S CHURCH HAS A FINE BEAMED ROOF, WHILE THE FONT BEARS THE MARKS OF HINGES WHEN IT WAS LOCKED TO PREVENT THE THEFT OF HOLY WATER FOR BLACK MAGIC RITES! THERE IS A SHOP, TEAROOM, BAKERY, POTTERY AND THREE PUBS: THE KINGS ARMS, CROWN AND WHITE ROSE. A TEMPERANCE HALL OF 1906 INCLUDES THE WCS.

Only slightly glimpsed – but very close by the walk – Nappa Hall is superb fortified manor house of the once influential Metcalfe family, and dates from the 15th century. It now operates as a farm, and in season a stunning display of snowdrops carpets the immediate wooded neighbourhood.

A major feature of this walk is the prospect of Addlebrough across the valley. At 1,575ft/480m this classic table-topped fell crops up in many Wensleydale views. Although obviously unseen from here, historic features abound in the form of a very distinctive Iron Age Brigante settlement on its flanks and a Bronze Age burial cairn on its summit: one is embellished with the cup-marks of these ancient people. Also here is the isolated large boulder known as the Devil's Stone, hurled by the Devil at Addlebrough's giant during a dispute.

Worton is a tiny village which includes the time-honoured Victoria pub (1698 date stone) and a house of 1729 bearing an inscription: 'MICHAEL SMITH MECHANICK BUT HE THAT BUILT ALL THINGS IS GOD Heb 3'. Dale House Farm bears a 1691 date stone. Further down the valley, the hamlet of Woodhall is strung along a short lane almost hidden in a surround of greenery. It has connections with the old hunting forest of Wensleydale.

Although the walk's two waterfalls occupy similar settings in deep, wooded gorges, their characters are vastly different. And each is of such quality that either would be a worthy focal point in its own right – we're just doubly blessed here. Whitfield Gill Force is a spectacular plunge into an impending amphitheatre. Though not as tall as the better-known Hardraw Force just up-dale, some of its aspects are finer, not least of all the fact that it's free! Contrastingly, Mill Gill Force tumbles delightfully over a mesmeric staircase of ledges.

THE BASICS

Distance: 8 miles / 12.75km

Gradient: Two undemanding uphill sections

Severity: Moderate

Approx. time to walk: 4 to 5 hours

Stiles: Eighteen

Maps: OS Landranger 98 Wensleydale & Upper Wharfedale; Explorer OL30 Yorkshire Dales North/Central

Path description: Fieldpaths and firm tracks, woodland paths near the end

Start Point: Askrigg village centre (GR SD 948910)

Parking: Roadside parking and car park at top end of village (DL8 3HT)

Dog friendly: Sheep pastures, so dogs on leads please, they should be fit and able to manage stiles

Public toilets: At start

Nearest food: Pubs and tearoom at start

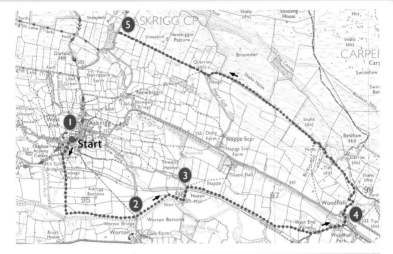

The Route

1. Follow the main road in the Hawes direction out of the bottom end of the village, and after the last house on the left take a track down the near side of an animal feeds works. Addlebrough's flat top breaks the skyline ahead. From the gate at the bottom pass between the supports of a former railway bridge, and the main track ends at a sewage works. Go straight ahead on a green track, through a gate/stile and further stiles to approach stepping stones on the Ure. Instead of following it to the very bank, go left on a low embankment to a small gate in a corner. Follow the fence away from it (parallel with the Ure) to a stile by a gate, from where the river is finally gained in predictably calm mood. Now accompany it downstream, a lovely stroll to emerge onto a road adjacent to Worton Bridge. The hamlet of Worton is a five-minute detour just across it, up the slope.

2. Without crossing the bridge, continue downriver from a stile opposite. After a pair of footbridges on Askrigg Beck and Newbiggin Beck in close succession the river bends off to the right, and you cross to a gate/stile at Nappa Mill Farm. Take the farm road left, re-crossing the old railway just before it crosses Newbiggin Beck by a stone-arched bridge and replacement.

3. Without crossing, take a gate/stile on the right and go right along the field bottom. During this spell there is a brief glimpse of the parapets of Nappa Hall a little further up the fields. At the corner a stile puts you onto the adjacent former railway line; simply head off along its grassy course. The river makes a splendid

appearance as a big sweeping arc that immediately meanders off again. Beyond a bridge in a small cutting (where the path veers slightly left onto the bank to avoid wetness) advance just a little further towards a blocked section. Here bear left to a footbridge onto a side-stream, and on to a stile out into a field corner. Bear gently left across to a gap-stile, and along to another ahead. Cross to another then along to a gate just to the right of a modern barn at West End Farm. Meeting an enclosed farm track, turn left up through the farm and through the hamlet of Woodhall before rising out onto the Carperby–Askrigg road.

4.   Cross straight over and pass between barns and a house opposite to take a farm track winding up the steep field. Addlebrough rises across the dale above the hamlet. Towards the top opt for the left fork, rising across to a gate/stile in a fence. It slants further up with a fence to a gate, then crosses a field centre to another gate into an area of grass-covered debris from lead mining. The track meanders through this to the right-hand of two gates opposite, beneath trees. With a wall on the left the track resumes along the edge of this colourful rough terrain, a lengthy spell that sees the track falter at sheep pens, but continue to a gate at the end. The track crosses an open pasture to another gate, to resume with a wall past more sheep pens and on to a final gate. Up above is the distinctive craggy edge of Broomber. The now enclosed track drops down onto a firmer enclosed track just above the house at Heugh. Turn right on this for a long and pleasurable level march to empty onto a narrow road climbing out of Askrigg.

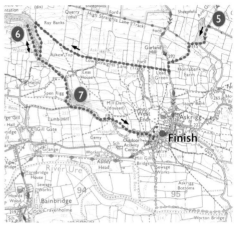

5. Turn down towards the valley, ignoring in turn a road left, a track right, and then the Muker road right. Just below is another walled track, and this you follow along to the right. Remain on this rough way, known as Low Straights Lane, to its very terminus, and here escape by a stile on the left; Whitfield Gill Force at once makes its presence known through the trees directly below. Your route must take a circuitous course in order to stand at its foot, for the steep slopes deter a direct descent. Instead the path heads downstream high above the wooded beck before dropping to a footbridge, then rises to meet the path to the waterfall. Turning upstream, care is needed as the final steps can be slippery underfoot. The scene is worth the effort, however, for this is a magnificent plunge.

6. To resume, retrace your steps to the junction and keep straight on the wooded bank top to a stile. The way then drops left through more open surrounds, crossing a bridleway and another stile and along to a stile out of the gill's confines, ignoring a footbridge just below. Advance on a couple of fieldsides outside the wooded gill's boundary wall, soon returning to the action at a stile ahead. The return path runs once more along the top of the steep, wooded bank, passing an old limekiln. A junction marks the detour to your second waterfall, Mill Gill Force: the situation is a near-replica of the one further up the beck. This time it is but a brief stroll along a firmer path upstream to witness the equally impressive falls.

7. After admiring the cascades return to the junction of paths and continue downstream on an excellent path on the top side of the wooded gill. The bonus of a distant view across Wensleydale is added to the charms of the gill itself. From a stile at the bottom of the wood another quickly re-enters to access a small footbridge on the beck. Just a short way downstream the path parts company with the beck to pass to the left of a mill conversion to a stile alongside. A neat, flagged path runs from here across the field to join a lane, which runs along to the left to re-enter Askrigg.

THIS WALK AMBLES AROUND THE GENTLE COUNTRYSIDE OF LOWER WENSLEYDALE, LINKING A MAJESTIC CASTLE WITH LOVELY VILLAGES. WHILE THE RETURN LEG AMBLES THROUGH A SERIES OF SHEEP PASTURES, THE OUTWARD ROUTE TAKES A SLIGHTLY ELEVATED COURSE THROUGH MORE OPEN COUNTRYSIDE, IN SPRINGTIME MUCH FAVOURED BY GROUND-NESTING BIRDS SUCH AS CURLEW AND LAPWING. THE WENSLEYDALE LANDMARK OF PENHILL DOMINATES THE SCENE ACROSS THE VALLEY.

Aysgarth is famous for its Upper, Middle and Lower Falls, where the Yoredale series of limestone makes its greatest showing to create a water wonderland in a beautifully wooded setting. By the Upper Falls is the graceful arch of Yore Bridge: Yore is the older name for the River Ure. Alongside is a cafe in a former spinning mill. Inside the commanding St Andrew's Church just up the hill are two fine 15th- and 16th-century screens, while just above that is the Aysgarth Falls Hotel. Aysgarth village stands high above the river, aloof from the natural attraction that brings visitors in their tens of thousands. It features the George and Dragon pub, a tearoom and stocks on the green.

Carperby is one of the most attractive villages in Wensleydale, its once greater importance evidenced by the market cross of 1674 on tiered steps at one end of the narrow green. At the opposite end is a group of places of worship which have been succumbing to modern trends: these include a Methodist chapel of 1820, a Wesleyan Chapel of 1880 and a Friends' Meeting House of 1864, also the old school. The Wheatsheaf was the honeymoon hotel of Alf Wight, better known as James Herriot, whose popular veterinary adventures were based around much of this area and neighbouring Swaledale.

Bolton Castle is a majestic ruin which on approach belies its ruinous state. This 14th-century manor house was converted into a castle by Richard, Lord Scrope, and Mary Queen of Scots was imprisoned here from 1568 to 1569. The labyrinthine interior is well worth exploring, with the addition of tearoom and gift shop. Other attractions include falconry displays and wild boars. Comprehensively overshadowed, Castle Bolton village is appealing in its own right. A spacious green separates two intermittent rows of cottages, many of which once housed lead-miners. Dating back more than 600 years, the little church of St Oswald stands almost at the castle wall.

THE BASICS

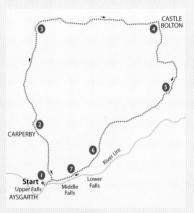

Distance: 7¼ miles / 11.5km

Gradient: Gentle rise in the early stages

Severity: Generally easy

Approx. time to walk: 3½ to 4½ hours

Stiles: Thirteen

Maps: OS Landranger 98 Wensleydale & Upper Wharfedale; Explorer OL30 Yorkshire Dales North/Central

Path description: Good field paths and firm tracks

Start Point: Aysgarth Falls National Park Centre (GR SE 011887)

Parking: National Park car park (DL8 3SR)

Dog friendly: Sheep pastures, so dogs on leads please, they should be fit and able to manage stiles

Public toilets: At start and at Castle Bolton

Nearest food: Pub at Carperby, tearoom at Bolton Castle

The Route

1. From the car park return to the road and turn left under the railway bridge. Just a few strides after the station yard take a hand-gate on the right into Freeholders' Wood. A good path rises through the trees, and just after a path comes in from the left, turn left on a good path forking left the few strides to a stile out of the wood. Head away to a wall-stile ahead, then bear right to a corner stile. Maintain this line to a stile part way along the wall on the right. Entering a larger field bear well to the right of an island barn to a corner stile, then turn left along the wallside to a stile onto a farm road, Low Lane. From a stile virtually opposite pass through a long, narrow field, through an old gateway to reach a stile/bridle-gate on the right at the end. Resume left through another slim field, bridging a tiny stream to a gate onto the road in Carperby opposite the Wheatsheaf.

2. Turn right a short distance past the village hall and head up Hargill Lane on the left. This rises out of the village to become a broad, walled track. On levelling out there is a glimpse across to Bolton Castle. A little beyond a barn it starts to climb away, and as it swings left in front of an old limekiln, instead fork right on a grassier, part-sunken track climbing by a wall. The way runs pleasantly on with the wall to a gate at the far corner into a large tract of colourful, rough pasture. A generally clear green track runs through the bracken of Bolton West Park, keeping left on the main way at a very early fork. Reaching a gate at the far end, the track runs on and you cross often-dry Beldon Beck on a sizeable bridge.

3. After the bridge the track runs through a vast pasture close by the right-hand wall. Take a gate in it just short of the corner – not the corner gate itself. The continuing improved track runs above the beck's replanted confines before passing through a gate in the left-hand corner to run more firmly alongside a wall to farm buildings. Continue on the access track through several fields towards imposing Bolton Castle, and through a belt of woodland the track leads to the very walls of the castle.

4.   Between church and castle you emerge onto the village street alongside the green, and from this corner descend the road out of the village. When it swings left part way down, continue straight down a drive past barns, descending to two houses and the defunct railway; in a small cutting stands the old station house. Across the old line a largely enclosed, leafy snicket drops down to join a road. Go left only as far as the Castle Bolton junction, then take a stile on the right. Cross to one at the far left corner of the long field, then bear right to another in the very bottom corner. Just below it is a stile onto Thoresby Lane at a stone slab footbridge on Beldon Beck. Along to the right the road quickly ends at Low Thoresby.

5.   At a gate to the right of the farm the lane is reborn as a super green path. Centuries old, its snaking route between hedgerows feels little altered. It finally terminates just beyond a wet junction with Watery Lane. A stream emerges from the field to run a part-channelled course over the lane; the left branch goes down to a ford and stepping stones on the Ure. From a gate/stile into a field a grass track follows the wall on your left to a gate/stile at the very far end, with High Thoresby over to the right. Rise gently away with the wall on your right as far as a stile in it (not used), then bear left over the brow to a stile near the far corner. A grassy path bears left to a gate onto a farm road; drop left down to Hollin House. Mighty Penhill is a major feature of the lower dale, and from this vicinity it is in particularly dominant mood.

6.   Drop down above the house, and maintain the slant on a grassy track down to a bridle-gate, and along the wallside to two neighbouring ones into a large, rolling pasture. There is a glimpse of Aysgarth church above the trees ahead, while you might hear the lower falls through the trees below. Cross to a bridle-gate into scattered Freeholders' Wood, from where a path runs by a fence on your right. Whilst this path runs straight ahead to join the firmly surfaced, hugely popular waterfalls path, part way on a grassy path drops directly left to a stile onto the terminus of the waterfalls path. Directly below you, a cleft in the cliffs permits a

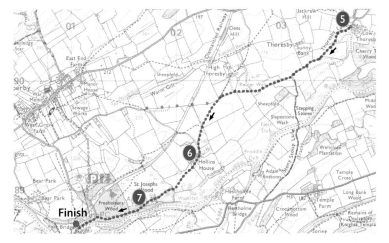

cul-de-sac descent to a slabby water's-edge vantage point for the Lower Falls. Back at the top of the cleft, a path runs along the short way to a hairpin bend of the main path, and keeping left this runs quickly upstream to the standard viewing point for the Lower Falls. Just a few strides further you emerge on the very riverbank alongside the falls; youngsters must be on a tight rein here!

7. Again just a few strides further, the path climbs back through the trees up to a gate to join the main path. Head left on this, entering denser woodland at a gate to quickly arrive above the Middle Falls viewing platform, down a few steps. Only a few strides further you emerge onto the road just below the car park entrance. To include the Upper Falls take the left-hand gate and turn down the road to Yore Bridge, from where a path then leads back up to the car park. Or for the car park, take the right-hand gate, crossing the road to a short-lived footway back up into the car park.

SWALEDALE IS AT ITS MOST COLOURFUL AND VIBRANT AROUND REETH, WHERE THE MAJOR SIDE VALLEY OF ARKENGARTHDALE JOINS THE SWALE IN THE SHADOW OF THE LONG, HIGH SKYLINE OF FREMINGTON EDGE. ADDITIONALLY, HARKERSIDE MOOR DOMINATES THE MAIN DALE ACROSS THE RIVER.

Reeth is focal point for the heart of Swaledale. It boasts an enviable position on the slopes of Calver Hill, well above the confluence of the Swale and Arkle Beck. It is to the latter of these two watercourses that Reeth shows allegiance, with Grinton claiming the Swale. Central is a large, sloping green, with the main buildings stood back on all sides. This old market town exudes a confident air, with hoary inns, shops and tearooms alongside the green: there is also a National Park Centre. Parking limitations can result in an untidy scene around the green in summer, amplified when market traders set up stalls on Fridays. Indelibly linked with the lead-mining days, Reeth was once much more populous. There is an absorbing folk museum, while annual agricultural shows and festivals add to its cultural attractions.

Arkengarthdale is the Swale's major side valley, and Arkle Beck is a fast-flowing, tree-lined tributary in keeping with its big brother. Rising on bleak moors near the Tan Hill Inn, it takes its name from Arkle Town, a tiny settlement south of Langthwaite, the 'capital' of the dale. This tiny village comprises two distinct sections. Along the through road a miscellany of buildings include St Mary's Church of 1819. The other half stands below the road, a cluster of houses grouped on the east bank of the beck. This attractive scene will be recognisable to older devotees of the televised veterinary adventures of James Herriot. In amongst these is the Red Lion, one of Arkengarthdale's two hostelries, a cosy little gem. The other pub is the CB Inn (named after one-time local landowner Charles Bathurst) which stands on the road beyond the church. Langthwaite was also the centre of the dale's lead-mining industry.

THE BASICS

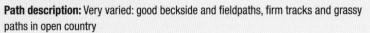

Distance: 9¾ miles / 15.5km

Gradient: Sustained climb near start, also a short climb to Booze

Severity: Quite strenuous

Approx. time to walk: 5 to 6 hours

Stiles: Twenty-five

Maps: OS Landranger 92 Barnard Castle & Richmond; Landranger 98 Wensleydale & Upper Wharfedale; Explorer OL30 Yorkshire Dales North/Central

Path description: Very varied: good beckside and fieldpaths, firm tracks and grassy paths in open country

Start Point: Reeth village centre (GR SE 038992)

Parking: Roadside parking in village centre (DL11 6TE)

Dog friendly: Sheep pastures, so dogs on leads please, they should be fit and able to manage stiles

Public toilets: At start and Langthwaite

Nearest food: Pubs and cafes at start; pub at Langthwaite

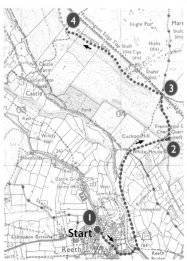

The Route

1. Descend the green and follow the road around to Reeth Bridge on Arkle Beck. Immediately after, take a stile on the left and take a wallside track left. When the track leaves go straight ahead to a gate at the end. Cross to the right of a barn ahead, and along to a stile at the end. Now  bear right to merge with the right-hand wall, and go along to a stile in it above a wooded bank. Leaving the valley floor, cross to a stile opposite then rise on a faint way past a barn to a gate/stile above. You will return to this crossroads. Now on the steep base of Fremington Edge take the thin path rising away, bearing slightly left to ascend near an old wall. This ascends steeply but pleasantly, enjoying a brief level halt. Here take the right fork, up a groove then gently up to a top right corner stile at the isolated White House.

2. A grassy way rises left through bracken to join a stony old road; turn left through a gate. A little further is the crest of Fremington Edge. The track swings sharp right at a guidepost, bound for the watershed wall ahead; at this point make use of Open Access as an inviting path runs left for a magnificent stride along the edge.

3. This will remain your course for the march to Fell End, with dramatic views across the valley to Calver Hill, with tree-lined Arkle Beck far below. The path varies in stature but remains largely clear. It rises gently to a substantial cairn amid mining remains, then on to the end of a sturdy wall on the edge.

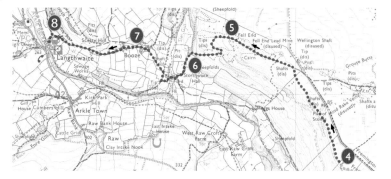

4. A stile sees you resume, all the way to pass through two crumbled walls. From the second the highest section at 1,510ft/460m is traversed to a redundant ladder-stile at a wall-end. Continue around this to a cairn, then a more pronounced drop works its way around the curving edge. Through more old workings the way drops more faintly to a ladder-stile in a wall, then over a broad grassy way and through a minor dip before the slightest of rises to a prominent cairn on Fell End. Here you are in the midst of much mining remains: steep, craggy ground drops away below.

5. To reach the valley, bear right to pick up a bridleway marked by regular cairns as it passes through Fell End Mine. Go left on this, dropping between a couple of old ruins. Booze is conspicuous across Slei Gill. As gradients steepen bear round to the left, dropping to the foot of a mine-ravaged gully, then swinging right to trace its edge down to a wall. Bear right with it to a gate just short of the corner. A green way descends a fieldside, becoming enclosed at the bottom to emerge at Storthwaite Hall.

6. Turn right along the front of the farmhouse out to a ford/ footbridge. Through the gate behind, follow the road just up around a bend until it passes through a gate. Ignoring this, instead turn right on a grassy path. Before reaching the wall ahead fork left off it, slanting up through a gateway to ascend steeply to the field top. Through  the right-hand gate Booze appears ahead. Cross the last field towards the nearest barns, passing through two gates to their left to join an access road in the hamlet.

7. Go left and follow this improving road slanting up past the houses, then running a level course before dropping steeply into the little square at Langthwaite.

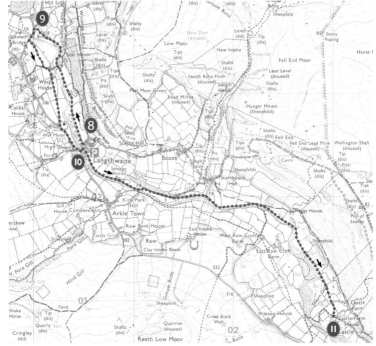

8. You will return to this point, but the up-dale loop begins by turning immediately right on a short, rough lane. From a gate at the end a path crosses a field, through a gateway to a stile at the end. The way continues on across two more fields to a house in front of Scar House, an imposing shooting lodge. Follow the drive down to join Scar House's drive, and head up it a few strides to locate a path through trees. Over a footbridge it emerges into a field. The thin path drops down nearer Arkle Beck, past a tiny barn to a stile into a large beckside pasture. This is crossed parallel with the beck to a stile onto a road at Stang Bridge.

9. Turn left on the road to Eskeleth Bridge. Before taking the second of two gates on the left, a short detour up the road reveals, just over the wall on the right, a hexagonal powder house from lead-mining days. Back at the gate a drive heads away past a house, with Scar House up to the left. Becoming enclosed it swings left towards Old School House; just before it take a stile on the right and a path crosses to join Scar House drive just ahead. Follow this right to emerge onto the

road at the church. A left turn sees a footway return through the rest of Langthwaite.

10. Turn left back down into the square, and right along a cart track to follow Arkle Beck downstream. It swings away from the beck to run beneath a wooded bank, then rises a little through the trees before swinging left at a fork; here take the footpath ahead, running to a stone-arched tunnel from mining days. Emerging, a path runs on near the beck past

mine ruins to a stile accessing a footbridge on Slei Gill. From the gate beyond, the path commences a delightful beckside stroll. Reaching a footbridge ignore it for the gate in front, after which your path breaks off the bridleway to remain in trees nearer the beck. This it does for some time until reaching a reedy area as the beck swings right. Avoid its excesses by keeping left, through an old wall and along to a gap in another. Skirt a moist corner the best you can, after which the way avoids the beck for some while. A faint, partly waymarked path rises gently above the beck, crossing the fields in a largely straight line aiming for prominent Castle Farm House ahead. Old walls in unkempt pastures are passed through, and a fence on the right also points the way until you rise more pleasantly to a stile in a wall ahead, then on one further small field to the house.

11. Pass to the left and on through collapsed walls just ahead, then cross to a prominent stile above a steep, scrubby bank. A path drops away, declining more gently though old walls and past a long-abandoned farm. Just beyond it the beck is rejoined, but on merging with a bridleway at an old gateway just ahead, the broad path forks left, ignoring a path dropping to the beck. After a short amble through trees

you emerge through a gateway amid colourful country. The broad path forges on alongside a fading wall on the right. After the second of two further gateways you curve round to the cross-paths on the outward route; through the stile on your right drop down past the barn to return as you came.

GUNNERSIDE, LIKE MOST OF ITS NEIGHBOURS, HAD ITS HEYDAY IN LEAD MINING TIMES, WHEN IT WAS A BUSY CENTRE FOR THE ONCE-THRIVING INDUSTRY. FOUNDED BY NORSEMEN, IT SEEMS GUNNAR WAS A VIKING CHIEF, AND UNTIL THE 1980s THE KINGS HEAD SPORTED A SUPERB PICTORIAL SIGN OF THE SAID INVADER.

The village shop and post office have been lost in recent times, but Gunnerside retains a tearoom/restaurant and the intriguing old smithy. The Literary Institute of 1877 serves as a village hall, and there is a Wesleyan Methodist Chapel of 1806.

The village straddles its own beck, which, apart from a level quarter-mile from here to the Swale, spends its time tumbling down the deep gill immediately above the village. Gunnerside Gill, even without its open-air mining 'museum', is arguably the most impressive in the Dales. For virtually four miles its steep sides sweep uninterruptedly down to the beck, with scale and colour of Lakeland proportions. The mines, however, add an extra element, and a gloomy day should be no deterrent to this walk. If anything, lingering cloud adds an almost tangible eeriness to the scene – assisted by the spirits of old miners, perhaps. The lead mines are as much a part of Swaledale as the waterfalls of Keld, and Gunnerside Gill is an excellent venue for their inspection.

At the turning point of the walk is Blakethwaite Smelt Mill, which served the mines. Built around 1820, its greatest surviving feature is the peat store, whose hauntingly ruinous form might be equally at home at Fountains Abbey. A semi-circular kiln sits high on the bank behind, where the old flue rose up the steep bank.

Ivelet is a hamlet in the shadow of Gunnerside Lodge, a shooting lodge of Lord Peel; all these surrounding moors are hallowed grouse-shooting territory. Ivelet Bridge is a beautiful old high-arched structure, without doubt the finest crossing of the Swale. On its near side is a flat stone slab on the ground: this was a coffin stone, used to rest the said item during the exhaustive funeral journeys that took place in Swaledale when the only consecrated ground was at Grinton. The building of Muker's church in 1580 was a major boon for mourners of the upper dale!

THE BASICS

Distance: 8 miles / 12.75km

Gradient: Two steady rises either side of Gunnerside Gill

Severity: Quite strenuous

Approx. time to walk: 4½ to 5½ hours

Stiles: Twenty

Maps: OS Landranger 91 Appleby-in-Westmorland (or 92 Barnard Castle & Richmond); Landranger 98 Wensleydale & Upper Wharfedale; Explorer OL30 Yorkshire Dales North/Central

Path description: Field paths and rougher paths and tracks in open country

Start Point: Gunnerside village centre (GR SD 951981)

Parking: Parking area on west side of bridge (DL11 6LE)

Dog friendly: Sheep pastures, so dogs on leads please, they should be fit and able to manage stiles

Public toilets: At start

Nearest food: Pub and tearoom at start

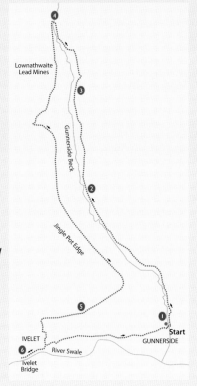

The Route

1. Leave the bridge by an access track on the pub side, following Gunnerside Beck upstream. After having been deflected around the grounds of Gunnerside Hall, small pastures lead a faint path along open surrounds until a stile puts you into a wooded bank of the beck. A clearer path now runs by the beck and a few boulders, on through a small gate and into denser woodland. A grand walk leads through this long sliver of woodland from where you rise above the beck. This early part of the walk through beautiful woodland contrasts strongly with the bleak scenes which will soon dominate. The wood is left in impressive surrounds as you near Gunnerside Beck again, dropping to a plank bridge out of the trees into an open strath; adjacent stiles send you along a wallside and through two further wall-stiles to reach the site of a crushing mill. A long row of bunkers just up behind was for storing lead ore.

2. Just past the ruins along this lawn-like flat pasture you reach a fence-stile. Here a path rises to run along a wallside to emerge above a steep bank dropping to the beck opposite a substantial ruin. This is a former mine 'shop', an office of the Sir Francis Mine. Here you leave the valley floor at a stile in the adjacent wall. An inviting, broad green path slants up through bracken, soon levelling out to shadow a wall along, parallel with the beck now far below. As the wall drops away the path rises again, absorbing another path at a cairn. As your path curves

up beneath a scar you suddenly find a dramatic scene of devastation greeting the eyes as the extensive lead workings at Bunton are revealed ahead. This is the site of another crushing mill, with another row of bunkers and many more features in evidence including a prominent level and hushes. In this section of the walk some classic hushes face each other across the gill. These were created by the release of previously dammed water which tore away the hillside in the search for new veins.

3.   Just beyond the last ruin in the immediate workings the path arrives at a staggered crossroads on a small knoll: the left fork slants down to the beck and follows it up the gill floor to Blakethwaite Smelt Mill, turning point of the walk. Amidst the ruins a large stone slab takes you over the beck. Any further exploration might include a couple of hundred paces' detour on a path up the west bank for a closer look at Blakethwaite Force (which is visible from the bridge). Enthusiasts can continue still further up the gill to the Blakethwaite mines and dams.

4.   From the smelt mill the return leg begins by crossing inflowing Blind Gill, from where a superb green way rises gently above the beck. Avoid any deviations and continue to rise to the day's last mining remains at Lownathwaite Mines, featuring North Hush. The path here surveys the many features of the walk's earlier mining sites from a splendid, detached platform. The track levels out before it contours around Botcher Gill to merge with a wide shooters' track. Going left, beyond Botcher Gill Gate it starts a gradual descent along Jingle Pot Edge, high above the enclave of Gunnerside Gill. Simply remain on the track as it eventually curves round to the right to slant down onto an open road above the cottages at Dyke Heads.

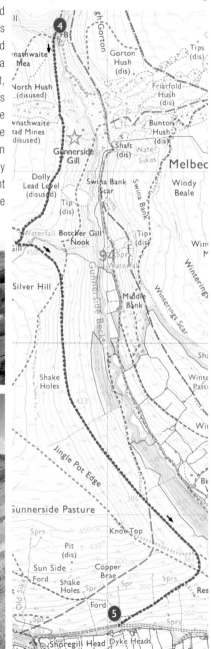

5. Turn right, enjoying the open views before the road drops down to bridge Shore Gill and up to a junction at Gunnerside Lodge. Turn left down the road into the hamlet of Ivelet. The final leg of the walk passes between buildings on the left by the phone box, but first continue just a little further down the road to the river, where just along to the right is the delightful Ivelet Bridge.

6. Back up the road in Ivelet, turn along the short-lived estate office access road by the phone box. A path quickly bears off right, dropping into trees to bridge Shore Gill before curving up to a gap-stile. Here begins a lovely final stage as the intermittent path steers a largely obvious course through numerous meadows. Head off through three intervening gap-stiles, then on past a spring to one just beyond the rear of an island barn. Through a further three stiles you arrive at a briefly enclosed section above the river at Marble Scar. Emerging, with Gunnerside just ahead now, drop down with the fence on your right almost to the bottom corner. Ignoring the stile, instead cross to a wall-stile to the left, then on through a gate and two further gap-stiles before crossing the final field to the nearest houses ahead. A little enclosed path runs between gardens to then follow the access road out into the village centre.

Upper Swaledale is Dales country at its finest, a particularly remote area where old haybarns are liberally dotted about flower-bedecked summer meadows. At its 19ᵗʰ-century peak, lead mining dominated this area, and the haunting remains of old mines, smelting mills and associated workings are scattered about the landscape.

Muker is a good centre for the upper dale, with the Farmers Arms and a shop/tearoom. This is probably the most picturesque village in the dale, with a fine grouping of buildings rising above Straw Beck. St Mary's Church was first built in 1580 to relieve Grinton's load, taking off its hands the God-fearing needs of the upper dale. The Literary Institute of 1868 is similarly prominent in front of it. The old school is now a crafts shop and gallery, and tablets proclaim that the famous Kearton brothers of neighbouring Thwaite were former pupils. The village pound where stray animals were held stands by the car park. Muker is the venue for the Swaledale Agricultural Show in September. The River Swale rejoins the main road below the village, after their enforced split by the island hill of Kisdon.

Keld is the first outpost of any size in Swaledale: beyond here are only isolated dwellings beneath the moors. Most of this Norse settlement is set around a tiny square just below the main road. The old Institute houses a Countryside and Heritage Centre, while refreshments are often available at Park Lodge. There is also a 'well-being garden' for quiet contemplation. A chapel of 1861 boasts a fine sundial, while the Great War memorial recalls four men who never returned to their farming hamlet. The fact that this delectable spot marks the junction of the Pennine Way and Coast to Coast Walk couldn't save its youth hostel from closure: today the former shooting lodge of Keld Lodge may be a more expensive replacement, but its presence has brought licensed premises back to Keld for the first time since the closure of the Cat Hole Inn in 1954.

Thwaite is a tiny village that long remains a happy memory to Pennine Wayfarers who descend to it from the long, lonely miles of Great Shunner Fell. The place they seek sanctuary from the open heath recalls another memory, that of local lads Richard and Cherry Kearton, who became pioneers in the early days of nature photography. The long-established Kearton Coffee House/shop makes a welcome place of refreshment.

THE BASICS

Distance: 7½ miles / 12km

Gradient: One notable uphill at Swinner Gill

Severity: Moderate

Approx. time to walk: 4 to 5 hours

Stiles: Thirty-five (though some are simple gaps)

Maps: OS Landranger 91 Appleby-in-Westmorland (or 92 Barnard Castle & Richmond) and Landranger 98 Wensleydale & Upper Wharfedale; Explorer OL30 Yorkshire Dales North/Central

Path description: Riverbank and field paths, some firm tracks

Start Point: Muker village centre (GR SD 910978)

Parking: Village car park in Muker (DL11 6QG)

Dog friendly: Sheep pastures, so dogs on leads please, they should be fit and able to manage stiles

Public toilets: At start and at Keld

Nearest food: Pub and tearoom at start; refreshments at Keld and Thwaite

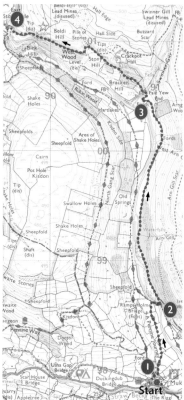

The Route

1. Leave the village centre by a road slanting up behind the Literary Institute at a triangular green. Pass to the right of an 'island' residence and then on past the former post office to a gate/stile out into a field. Initially a track, by the first gate/stile this becomes a well-defined, stone-flagged path crossing seven fields linked by solid stiles to arrive at the bank of the River Swale. Turn right to another stile to follow the Swale downstream the few strides to Rampsholme Bridge. This tall footbridge is the only crossing of the Swale between Keld and Ivelet Bridge and makes an excellent viewpoint for the lonely Swale Gorge, as far upstream as the cleft of Swinner Gill.

2. On the opposite bank drop down left to the river and soon a wide track is joined. On crossing the first inflowing beck, stroll a short distance up its course for a fine view of the charming waterfall of Arn Gill Force tumbling through foliage. Continuing,

the track rises a little above the river to run on to cross a bridge below the ravine of Swinner Gill. The steep-sided gill above your crossing was once a thriving lead-mining scene.

3. The track then rises steeply before easing out above an increasingly impressive wooded, rocky gorge. A track from the ruin of Crackpot Hall is joined, and this same track runs left on above a steep, fenced scree slope into the gorge beneath Beldi Hill before descending to a stone-arched bridge over East Gill. Here the way forks; first take a few strides on the left path to appraise East Gill Force directly beneath you.

4. Resume on the right branch, a cart track rising steeply but quickly to East Stonesdale Farm. On entering the yard turn left above the house and follow its access track all the way out to join the Tan Hill road. En route this largely level promenade enjoys open views over Keld beneath you. The track bridges Stonesdale Beck (with Currack Force off-path 100 yards downstream) before climbing to the road. Turn left down this with its steep little hairpin to cross a bridge on the Swale alongside a junction and lone house.

5. While your onward route is left, first go very briefly right to view Wainwath Force beneath the limestone cliffs of Cotterby Scar. Turning left along the road, it leads quite quickly to Keld. Take the first turning left to drop down into the square.

6. Leaving Keld, keep left this time to climb back to the main road by Keld Lodge, and turn left out of the village. A little beyond a bridleway on the left a stile will be found. Drop down a little and cross to a stile ahead. Here begins a field path marked by regular stiles; in early summer these flower-rich meadows ensure a delectable path. Early on, where you don't see a stile, simply cross to a footbridge on a side-stream to resume. A further guide is a string of field barns all passed on their right. A brow beneath the hamlet of Angram reveals Thwaite with Lovely Seat above' to your left Kisdon's western flank looks splendid.

7. The road is rejoined at a stile after skirting Angram, and within a couple of minutes is vacated again at a gate/stile on the left. Slant down to find a stile beyond an island barn, then on to bridge a stream. Through a stile just beyond, follow the left-hand wall away through several pastures. At a stile by a barn the wall ends and you cross to another stile/barn at the end. A moist corner leads on, now alongside tree-lined Skeb Skeugh. A part-flagged path runs to a corner stile, then an embanked path bears left to another corner stile. Continue on through a gate/stile, and left of some barns to a gate/stile onto an enclosed path, turning right into the huddled village of Thwaite.

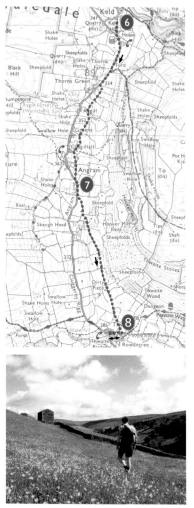

8. Returning to the point you entered Thwaite, this time keep straight on the enclosed path. Two stiles in quick succession lead into a field. Here the Pennine Way strikes left, but you continue with Thwaite Beck to a wall-stile ahead. Here leave the beck for a thin path across three further fields, in the second of which you follow a wallside. At the end you converge with Skeb Skeugh again, coming in from the left. It is crossed on a stone-arched footbridge. From a stile just beyond, head away with a wall to a corner stile at the end, then pass right of a barn to a wall-stile from where a beckside path joins the road at Usha Gap Bridge.

9. Go briefly left along the road and then go left to the farmhouse at Usha Gap. Turn right through the farmyard to a gate into a camping field, then bear left to find a wall-stile near the far end. From here a string of obvious wall-stiles lead a faint path across the field-bottoms to Muker, already waiting ahead. In the final field the path is flagged. Emerging into the village, a little pathway on the right drops down to emerge alongside the pub.

ABOUT THE AUTHOR

Paul Hannon is Yorkshire born and bred, and has been writing about his native county for over 30 years. He has produced around 80 guidebooks to walks in his own and neighbouring counties Lancashire and Cumbria, as well as cycling and general guides, and has contributed to numerous magazines.

A keen photographer, he is currently making greater use of his extensive photographic archive to develop an exhaustive picture library dedicated to all things Yorkshire.

A father of three grown-up children, he still lives in his hometown of Keighley. When not walking and photographing, his interests include Bradford City FC, ornithology and good beer.

As a serious hillwalker he has climbed hundreds of mountains in the British Isles. In 1991 he completed the 214 Lake District 'Wainwright' fells, and became a proud Munroist on completing the 284 Scottish 3,000-foot peaks on his 50th birthday.